When the Church Thinks You're Crazy

One woman's journey from abuse and
toxic relationships to freedom

Bethany Elle

ISBN: 979-8-9919424-1-6

Dedication

To my loving and devoted husband, and each of my five children, daughters-in-laws, and grandchildren.

Thank you for being my sunshine, even in the darkest of days.

To my Heart-Mom, Bunnie.

To my favorite all time teacher, Colleen.

Acknowledgments

I would not be the woman I am today if it weren't for the loving pursuit of God and His amazing grace in my life.

I am forever thankful for the loving support of my dearest friend, Bunnie. Thank you for being there for me for most of my life. You are now in heaven, but still in my heart.

My girlfriends, Marie, Kathy, Annette, Sherilyn, Marie S, Laura, Leslie, and sweet Alyssa. Thank you for being in my life. I value each one of you so much and am abundantly blessed by your friendships. We enjoy many good times together, and I wouldn't want to do life without you.

My son, for his excellent photos.

About the Author

Bethany Elle is a best-selling author, national speaker, and a certified identity trauma coach. She is the founder and director of a non-profit ministry for woman, Agape Celebration.

She is the mother of five, grandmother to six and married to her college sweetheart for over 40 years.

Bethany's mission is REAL:

Rooted.Empowered.Authentic.Loved.

She chooses to be a light to all those around her, to live a life of hope through adversity, help others understand their identity, and to leave a legacy for her family and friends.

Preface

When the Church Thinks You're Crazy is a revised and expanded version of my first book, I Am Real. I decided to rewrite my memoir with the idea of adding more details and, with permission, using some of the correct names for the characters involved. Healing is a process, writing my memoir is part of that process, and God uses my story to help others heal as well.

The experiences you will read in this book are my own. Some of them have been altered for protection purposes, and the names of some mentioned have been changed. Not every experience or person that I've interacted with is mentioned. I want to acknowledge that a few have impacted my life immensely and in a positive way. Yet, I did not bring them into this story. My hope for this book is to give any reader that has experienced spiritual, emotional, or sexual abuse a glimmer of hope.

This book shows God's immense power and the incredible healing that takes place when we learn to believe who we are according to God. I share my journey of trauma and allow you to see how God took it all and grew me into someone different.

I hope that by reading this book, you will understand the impact we have on each other. And that it will give you a desire to be gently invested in kindness. This book is an expansion of my first book, I Am Real/BE Unmasked. You, the reader, have the power to encourage, empathize, self-reflect, and love your own journey and the one I am sharing with you. Please handle them both with care.

Thank you for investing the time to discover.

Contents

Chapter 1

My mind often wanders back to days long gone. I'm a young mother with three little boys 4, 2, and a newborn. I don't really know *how* to be a mother, but here it is every day whether I know how or not.

I meet my husband in college, in a crowded classroom. He sits on one end of the row of seats, I sit on the other. We both lean forward at the same time and smile at each other. It's all history from there.

I don't have a reason academically to be in college. I'm smart, but I don't care about studying. It's so boring. However, there's no other place to be right now, so I'm here in a classroom learning about marriage and family. The truth is, I want to find a husband with a good career that will love me and treat me with kindness. I'm ready to get married.

I think everything is pretty good in my life. I grew up with the only religion that gets people to heaven. My mother is a single hard -working woman that tried her best, and my brothers love me. I don't expect much but hope for a lot.

Now that a third baby, another boy, has come along it feels like an ambush. It feels like something inside of me is off, but I can't pinpoint what it is. I'm sad. I scold myself for thinking such a thing. Look at me, great husband, healthy sons, beautiful home, two cars, and the life many women dream of. Why on earth do I feel sad? Maybe sad isn't the right word; it's scrambled. I feel chaotic, scrambled, lost, alone. I do notice that I forget more things now and I'm tired, but hey, I'm a mom of three young boys. I'm supposed to be tired!

A tumbling thought breaks in before I have a chance to demolish it. I feel myself getting dizzy and my mind wanders as a way of protection. I scramble to stay present, while at the same time I don't want to be present for this thought:

**

A little girl runs down the hallway, her shoulder-length reddish brown hair whipping around her face. She couldn't have been more than nine years of age. Gasping and sweating, she runs down a long hallway.

The grey walls of the hallway suffocate her. She feels stuck in a hamster-wheel like she can't escape it even if she tried. Her shadow grows larger behind her, like a monster ready to eat her up. But the real monster is running behind her, looming darker than the shadow. Tears run down her face in rivulets as she tries to push her legs faster. She curses her lack of stamina in her head as she keeps trying to outrun the monster behind her.

The monster makes no sound but advances toward her. The little girl feels like she will pass out, her blue dress with the white lace that she loves so much is twisted around her body. She feels trapped – lost and afraid. The fear is so overwhelming that it feels like it might swallow her whole, and she will never resurface from its pits. She sees a man's

dark silhouette coming at her. The little girl whimpers out of
fear.

***

My cup crashes to the floor and I silently swear under my breath. Coffee seeps into the carpet and I rush to get a cloth to clean it up.

The ringing of laughter from my two boys in the playroom, and my youngest crying in his room, diverts me back to my reality and I race to ease my newborns discomfort. I put a hand on my chest and feel my heartbeat race a mile a minute. My body is covered in a sheen of sweat, and my head is fuzzy from the sudden onslaught of intense thoughts. I remember my mother told me that day to go with Jared to his BYU campus. Jared is a friend of hers, and he wants me to see his campus. I am maybe nine at the time, so I do as she requests.

But now, I begin to question myself. Did it really happen? Or did my mind make that all up? It doesn't seem logical that my mother would just let her nine-year-old daughter go with her friend to his college alone. The old fear still makes my heart race and hands shake, making me think otherwise. The memory feels unequivocally real, though it transcends logic. Thoughts of doubt trample over any reality and I once again scold myself for coming up with such dramatic lies. How do I think of these things, and why? I ask myself.

Before my heart settles down, I am inundated with more flashes of memories. Little glimpses of what was quite possibly my life race through my mind. *Running. Cowering. Hiding.* My voice is strangled from calling out. My headache intensifies. The images are all jumbled up, and I cannot make sense of them, except that they paralyze me with fear and pain.

My day continues to be a mixture of invading thoughts, vicious scolding, and pervasive shame. I don't have words for any of it, I just think I am living in an imaginative world of violence and tell myself it must be from watching the path of my two older brothers. They were both involved in drugs and spent time in and out of jail. They brought their hippie friends home to our house to spend the night and smoke weed. Police patrolled our house on a regular basis watching for them and waiting to haul them back to jail. I console myself with thoughts of being better than them. I don't do drugs, or drink alcohol. In fact, I keep all the Seventh Day

Adventist rules, which means I'll be in heaven for sure. Unless of course God considers these stories in my mind lies, then I'm doomed.

This is my life. Three rambunctious boys, a loving husband, and a running movie in my mind of nothing I can remember. Unless this is remembering?

My journal is full of questions: *Why is it so hard for me to remember being a kid? What was it like being 7, 8, or 9? When did we live in that single wide trailer? Did I have a bedroom? Did I ever meet my dad? What is my real name? What are these thoughts about, and why can't I just think about true things? What is true? Who is God? Why is he so angry with me? Am I even real? Do I really want to be an Adventist? How do I know for sure it's the truth?*

I pound out the questions, one after another on the papers of my pink flower journal. I pretend with my boys that I'm making fancy lines on the paper as they watch me scribble letters they don't yet understand.

The thoughts, which I later learn are flashbacks, become more vivid with time. More questions pile up about my life and myself, as I stubbornly try to combat each thought with a scornful scolding and another question about who I am. It feels like I'm living someone else's life. I am a puppet, controlled by the past images that take over my mind at random moments. I begin to doubt what I believe to be real in my life. On some level I begin to separate what was and what is. My life as of present has all the ingredients of a content and happy life, even though nothing too exciting ever happens in our town, except for the time my mom decides I am missing, and the police show up at our door with their guns drawn. Oh, and the time my mom decides I am in some sort of trouble so, again, she calls the police, and I am terrified when they bombard my back yard with flashlights and bang on the door. Those times are exciting!

My journal becomes a life saver throughout the day as I scribble my own thoughts. The boys color and play with their crayons, cars, and superheroes.

Running. Trapped. Hotel. Man. Shame. Secrets.

With each demoralizing thought I spiral into the pit of shame. I feel trapped in the cage of my own body, silent screams just waiting to burst through, but nobody can hear my cries for help. Tears flow easily and I attempt to explain to my husband the convoluted thoughts that persistently invade me. But, to no avail, I am usually at a loss for words unless I have a pen in hand and my journal ready.

Something inside of me is starving, a journal entry explains, *I wonder how I can know if I'm real, or if God is real, or if anything around me is real?*

Later that night after the boys are safely tucked away, I find myself with a razor in one hand and blood streaming down the other arm. I feel panic and calm at the same time, panic because I'm bleeding, it hurts and I'm not sure what I just did. Calm because I feel like this is evidence of being real. I need to know. If I'm real, then maybe the thoughts in my head are real too and I'm not making them up. Maybe there is something to this crazy randomness. Maybe it's possible to have a happy life now, and still have thoughts of severe pain and abandonment from years gone by. Maybe I can figure this out.

I write in my journal: *The person I think I should be, the one I think people want me to be is slipping away. I don't want to be that person for the rest of my life; I don't believe the stuff I've been told. I do not want to raise my children in a cage. I do not fully understand the images that race through my mind. I can be cooking in the kitchen, and suddenly, I see myself as a young girl with a man on top of me. Or I'm running down a hallway desperately trying to escape someone or something. I'm in a truck with a man. Or I'm sitting in front of a man, and he is fondling himself. I feel like I need a beginning, a way to define myself outside of the family I grew up in.*

It occurs to me one afternoon while making lunch for the boys that maybe I don't feel real because so many things about childhood are uncertain. I'm not certain about who my father is or what my last name was as a child. I'm not certain about the faith I grew up in. I'm not certain if I like the first name my mother gave me or why she chose it. Her story is that she named me Sharon after her sister's stepdaughter Sharon. So, we had Big Sharon and Little Sharon. Her intention before I was born was to give me her favorite name which was Rebeka. She loved that name as she grew up and always wanted a daughter named Rebeka. But because I was born on Big Sharon's birthday, I got the name Little Sharon.

I begin to toy with the idea of a name change. Why not, right? People change their last names, so why not the first name too? I decide quickly that my middle name will stay the same; it's after my maternal grandmother, and I like it. I announce to my husband that I've decided to change my first name. It's a first step for me in discovering who I really am. He takes the news in stride and joins me in exploring the different options.

Sarah, Elizabeth, Brooklyn, Amy, Bethany, Morgan, Jane. The list grows over the next few days as I try each one on and imagine myself living with a new name. I feel excited about the idea and begin to research the legalities of such a change.

This could be the beginning of many changes, I ponder. What if I go all out and get my ears pierced? Buy jewelry and wear a wedding ring? All these things were strictly forbidden to me as a child growing up as an Adventist. I could be an entirely different person someday; I could be free! I remember my first necklace. My brother gave it to me. I still have it in my drawer; it's a large blue glass gem. As a child I hung it on the post of my bed and dreamed about wearing it, but it never did make it around my neck.

I am afraid. What if everything I've been told is true? Wearing a ring could send me straight to hell? If I change my name, I can't go back. I will have to learn who I am. What if the images in my mind are simply a figment of my imagination? How can I know the truth of what is happening?

I settle on the name Bethany. It has a couple of different meanings. 1) Fig leaf and 2) House of God. I like them both. I recall the story of Adam and Eve in the garden after they eat the forbidden apple and discover their nakedness. They make themselves coverings out of fig leaves and it helps them feel better about their shame. And then, there's Bethany a town where Jesus often visited friends. He went there to rest and be restored, laugh, and eat. It all sounds so comforting to me, so safe.

My husband likes my choice, and we proceed with the next step. I have paperwork to fill out and I take my paperwork before a judge and ask him to sign it. Just like that my name is legally changed with the signature of some man I don't know!

The judge, an older man in a room decorated with floral carpet and rich wooden walls and a desk asks me why I'm changing my name.

"I don't like it or the reason I was named Sharon." I answer honestly.

"That is courageous. Okay, I will sign this form for you, and from now on, you will legally be called Bethany. Enjoy your new name!" He hands me the form with his signature scrawled on it, giving me a friendly smile.

"That was easy!" My husband, Cliff, comments as we leave the courthouse.

"Feels like I finally did something for myself. I feel brave. It's another step towards what I am searching for. Freedom, hope, stability, and identifying who I truly am," I respond.

My answer hangs in the air between us as we sit in the car together, we don't know what the next step will bring.

When we come back home, I cannot help but think about my childhood. Changing my name brings back memories. I think of how my last name wasn't my own. It was my stepfather's name that I took on even though it wasn't legally my name. I searched for my birth father my entire life, but he had ditched my mother and me. It was just my mother and my three brothers, one of whom got murdered, and one that was abusive. The third one was the perfect golden boy, and then there was me — invisible and different from everyone else.

My mother didn't give me my biological father's name. I didn't know him or my origins.

I feel like I live in a question mark. My own name isn't my identity but borrowed from people I don't know. It's more proof of how I feel, nonexistent in the minds of others, including myself. My stepfather seemed like an okay guy but taking on his name felt awkward. I believed the lie that I did not exist just like my biological name did not exist.

People automatically thought that I was from an affluent family because of my stepfather's last name, but when they learned the truth, I would be pushed aside as if I never existed. All the class differences and judgment I faced as a child just because I wasn't rich or popular enough only confirmed to me that I was insignificant. I feel inner turmoil over my name. The flashbacks and fears hide me from recognizing the deeper root. Several families with the same name grew up with me. We were friends, but there was still the feeling of being lesser than. The feeling of being invisible dominated my existence in the presence of prominence.

It's an adjustment to have a new first name. I keep thinking of myself as Sharon and then consciously switch over to Bethany. Friends may think it's weird, but they comply and work hard to call me Bethany. My family feels hurt. My mother doesn't understand why I did such a thing and doesn't easily change to my new name. My brothers tried, but they too slip into the natural name of Sharon. It takes years before they all adjust and call me by the name I have chosen, Bethany.

I begin to contemplate all the rules we have in church and how so many of them don't make sense to me. I question the Adventist prophet, Ellen G. White, and decide I'm not going to read her books anymore. I toil with the thought that God is angry with me, and He is sitting up in his heavenly realm on his golden throne just waiting for me to mess up. I believe that when I do mess up, He is right there erasing my name from the Book of Life. I feel like I'm constantly walking on the line between heaven and hell, and I'm ready to get off the line.

Cliff and I discuss the pros and cons of Adventism. He too grew up as a Seventh Day Adventist and believes that he is in the right church with the right people to go to heaven. He believes all the stuff Ellen G. White wrote about and the sermons we hear every Saturday. He feels that keeping

Saturday sacred is a matter of life and death and the Adventist belief of what happens after death is imperative. He doesn't see God as angry like I do. God may not exactly be in a good mood, but he is nice enough.

I ponder my belief about the Book of Life and question in my journal:

How can I be valuable if I am so easily erased?

My life is invisible. I feel like a bottomless pit with no purpose or goal in mind. Something inside of me is gnawing and clawing to break free, yet here I am at a holding point. I am searching for something. The gaps in my mind float away, out of reach, unseen and unknown.

These thoughts plague me, and I wonder if there is a way to escape them. Can I break away from these thoughts? They spill out on the well-worn tear-stained pages of my journal as I ponder over the concept of my freedom from the shackles of misery and constrictions of my childhood. I know something must change; somehow, I need to change. Of course, the thought of change brings with it a certain amount of uncertainty. Will changing make anything better? According to the church that I grew up in, changing will buy me an all-access pass to hell. But I want my children to grow up without any of the constraints or limitations that I had to endure.

My life is beautiful on the outside; if not for the lurking shadows and demons that haunt my mind, I can say it is perfect. We married at a young age Cliff 21 and I was 19, we have three beautiful sons. After giving birth to my firstborn, I want more than anything to give my children a happy childhood. I want them to have a fulfilling life with safety and happiness. And seeing them thrive makes me more determined to protect them and their happiness.

"I don't remember being happy as a kid like our kids," I muse one day. "I don't remember having good times, or even feeling safe and free enough just to be myself."

Cliff doesn't understand this concept. He was the youngest of three children. His sister was the oldest, then his brother. Ten years later, Cliff came along. His parents knew he was special, and they favored him above all else. He was spoiled.

"I want our boys to grow up never having to feel ashamed, invisible, or afraid to be themselves."

"They will" Cliff consoles. They know we love them, and we are going to figure this all out.

"I feel like there is stuff that happened in my childhood that I'm just not clear about. I recognize that I am missing large gaps in time, that I am completely blank on what happened. I don't know how to fix it," I say, my words a bit muffled as I snuggle into his shoulder. I know my body and mind display symptoms of trauma; it doesn't make sense. I can't be sure any of it is real. I question everything I see in my mind.

I want to change not just for myself but for my family and their well-being. I know I will have to throw out all the old beliefs I was raised with. The idea of doing this is paralyzing and liberating at the same time.

"A friend of mine has been seeing a Christian psychologist. She recommended him to me." I say, pulling back to fully look at him.

"That's an interesting idea" Cliff answers. "Do you think that will be helpful?"

"Yes," I reply with a slight tremble in my voice. Nevertheless, I feel confident in my answer and decision. It brings me hope.

The same night, I force myself to lock my pain away inside my journal. I don't have to think about it tonight because if I do, the feelings will drown me, and I can't let that happen. I am afraid. I feel that if I show anyone the real intensity and severity of it all, no one will believe me. They will call me silly, liar, or a drama queen. I will feel more invisible. I will be left all alone. And loneliness is worse than any other feeling in the world.

Chapter 2

We gather in the living room to watch the boys play. Unfolded laundry takes one cushion on the couch, and I chastise myself for not getting it all done earlier in the day. The boys are happy with their cars, superheroes, and music. They all chatter at once competing for our attention. My mind is working overtime to focus on them and to also block the graphic images and thoughts that barge their way in. I am bombarded by images and memories that don't seem real. It feels like my mind skips time to make everything work properly. I recognize that I forget things I've said or done and the hours in the day go by much quicker than they should. This is crazy, I think to myself. How can I confirm the images in my head when I can't even keep track of my day? What can I do to accurately remember my childhood, and do I really want to know? The boys squeal with joy as Cliff bounces them up and down on his feet and they tumble from the couch to the floor. I smile at them and help them get to their feet each time. I know I'm not fully present, I don't know what to do about it.

I chide myself for not remembering or knowing what is real. The figures that methodically starve my time seem to belong to someone else. Wouldn't I remember such disturbing and dark things if they happened to me? It feels like I'm in a deep sleep for a long period of time and then I wake up without having any memories of anything that happened in my previous life. My feelings and thoughts get mixed up, and I am unsure of what is true and false.

"I made an appointment with that psychologist today" I mention to Cliff as the boy's whiz by with their superhero capes flying behind them. "It's tomorrow." I say with reservation.

"Oh! That was fast!" Cliff says out of breath as he swings one boy at a time around the room.

The next morning, I get the boys settled in the TV room with their favorite show on. I think back again to my own childhood when I would sit on the floor next to my grandfather and watch TV. I loved Bonanza, Little House on the Prairie, and the Brady Bunch. Those were our shows, the ones we watched together. The doorbell rings and I let the babysitter in. She's a sweet girl and the boys have a lot of fun with her. I show her the lunches I've packed in the refrigerator and tell her I'll be back in about 3 hours. I'm going to run a few errands while I'm out.

I sit in the waiting area feeling a little nervous and out of place. I'm not sure what to expect. An older man approaches me, he is of medium build with a buzz cut. His blue eyes twinkle and he is nicely dressed. "Bethany?" He asks. "Yes." I hold out my hand to shake his. "Hi, I'm Frank; it's nice to meet you. We will be meeting in my office which is down this hall." He points ahead and starts to walk towards his office door. "Can I get you anything to drink?" he offers.

"No thank you." I say absently. My mind is already scanning the room. I know all the escape routes, how the window opens, where the best seat is for a quick escape, and where the clock is. I cautiously take a seat and look at him questioningly.

"When we talked on the phone, you mentioned that you've been struggling with invasive thoughts. I'd like us to talk about that in the next few weeks, but first I think it will be nice to get to know each other a little." He puts his coffee cup down on the table beside his chair and crosses his legs with his hands folded in his lap. "Do you want to share a little about your life right now?" he asks.

I clear my throat, "Sure" I say "I'm married now for about eight years, we met in college. I have three little boys, the youngest is just a couple months old. They keep me super busy." I smile and begin to relax a little more as I think about my three little guys. "Can I ask you a few questions?" I venture.

"Sure," Frank replies, "you can ask me anything you want."

I sit forward a little as if that might bolster my courage. "Hmm," I think out loud "how long have you been practicing? And are you a Christian?"

"I've been in practice for over 20 years." he says proudly. "And, yes, I am a Christian."

"Do you have a family?" I'm curious.

"I do. I have two teenagers who will soon be headed off to college. They grow up fast!" He shakes his head as if he's remembering when his kids were just little like mine.

"Do you attend church?" I wonder if it's okay to ask him

that. "I do." He says easily. "We are currently looking for a new church to attend. My kids are wanting something that has more to offer for their age group."

He answers all my questions patiently, and I continue drilling him. I want to be sure he is someone I can trust because if I'm going to share the crazy in my head, I want to know I can trust him. By the end of our first session, my questions are complete. I feel hopeful. He seems like he can help me figure out what is going on inside my head. Before leaving his office, we set up appointments every week. I realize that I look forward to our future 50-minute sessions where we can hopefully get to the bottom of these disturbing memories and thoughts.

That evening, I go over the details of my visit with Cliff and we discuss the hopeful feeling. Neither one of us has been to therapy before or heard much about it, so it's all new to us. I decide that I will tell Cliff about each session and move forward with whatever happens, even when it's hard.

In the first few months of therapy my sessions revolve around the subject of family. As they are the center of my universe, it makes sense to start with them first. They are also one of the biggest reasons and motivations for me to get help. Frank tells me more about his own family too. He says he's been married for 20 years and grew up in the area. He lives in the country in a house they built, and he has a dog.

I like talking to him, but I carefully avoid anything too deep. I am still hesitant about trusting him with my secret, the stuff that brings on that feeling of shame, discontent, fear, and craziness. I am careful not to be too vulnerable. He doesn't push me, but also makes it clear to me that he is there to listen to whatever I want to say. He has an easiness about him that relaxes me, and I ponder whether trusting him is worth it to me.

We start discussing my choices in life when it comes to my family. I tell him about how I chose to be a stay-at-home mom and give my children a consistent childhood. I want them to be happy, with a mother and a father they can count on. I didn't grow up with a father, and so my early life was full of uncertainty. I don't want my children to go through something like that.

I share my need to protect my kids and give them a life full of hope because I didn't have those things either. I tell him about how I always felt awkward, lost, invisible, and unwanted. After a couple of months, he starts to probe me for more, asking me to share more about my childhood. The more questions he asks, the more my mind twists up. With each probe I feel fear, anguish, shame, and I wonder if he will tell me to leave his office. I grasp for the right words to begin to share something, but instead I feel blocked and confused.

I explain to him that when I think of my childhood, there seems to be large gaps of time, and only bits and pieces come back. The fragments fill me with questions, confusion, and fear. It is challenging to talk about them. The memories and feelings strangle my voice, filling me with dread, unable to do or say anything while I sit on his couch. He asks me about my reasons for changing my name, and how I feel about the church I grew up in.

Months pass by as I grapple with the incessant search for words that refuse to formulate in my mind as if threatened by some unknown force or entity. I cannot pinpoint the origin of angst, but the vigilant threat is palpable and paralyzing. Then, Frank asks me about the visions and flashbacks I keep getting. He asks me about the confusion regarding those visions and memories. After mentioning the one flashback I have of running in the darkened hall, trying to escape from someone chasing me down, he asks me to elaborate. He takes me back to the memory and tries to help me remember more about that incident.

"Let's try something that will help you relax today. Maybe it will help you talk," he starts.

I sit across from him on the soft brown couch that envelops my body like a cloud, but, on the inside, I am stiff as a board. He moves from the chair and sits beside me on the couch.

"Think of a place that relaxes you. Someplace that you love, somewhere that calms you down," he says.

The vision of a crystal-clear aqua ocean comes to my mind. The water has a calming sound, sparkling under the sun, and clear enough to paint an almost kaleidoscopic image of the reefs and wildlife below the surface. I tell him about what I see, and he says, "That's great. Now, watch the waves as I count."

He starts to count, and I listen. The higher the numbers go, the more I begin to calm down. I can feel my body relax; the tense muscles loosen. My mind feels soothed and slowly emptied of fear. I sink deeper into the couch, my breathing slow and steady. I hear his voice in the background as I imagine myself on this beautiful beach with the warm sun streaming down on me. The waves wrap around my feet in a comforting swirl.

"Now, I want you to know that you are completely safe here. Nothing and no one can hurt you. It's just you here in the sand at peace. I want you to go back a little and think about when you were a child. Think about the time when you were running down that dark hallway. Tell me if you can remember anything more," he said, his breathing mirroring mine.

I can feel my mind stretching back over the years. I feel resistance deep within and the urge to clench into protective mode, but I give in to the images that plod before me, like a movie on a tiny screen, unbidden and disregarding the fears that wish to push them away.

I see myself as a child of around eight or nine years old, standing near the end of the long hallway. I see a tall young man standing by me. I recognize him as Jared, my mom's friend from BYU. I can feel what I was feeling at that moment. Afraid, confused, and caged. Then, I remember running away from him in the dark hallway - the hallway that seemed to go on forever. As soon as I begin talking about it, it feels real. It feels like it is happening in real-time.

I feel like I have gone back in time, one feeling tumbling upon another. As soon as I recognize Jared's face in my memory, I tense up again.

"What do you see?" Frank prods

"I can see a man who's with me at the end of the hall," I tell Frank. "He was a friend of my mother's and a university student. She…she sent me with him that day."

It starts getting harder to breathe, and the fear rises like hot lava within me. I can feel tears stream down my face burning my cheeks with a salty stream of distress.

"Get me out!" I cry out, the fear running over me like a flood.

Frank starts counting the waves again, "Ten, nine, eight, seven, six, five, four. Come back to this room now, Bethany. You will feel relaxed and safe. Three, two, one."

He reaches out and grabs my hand, comforting me. After that day, the sessions continue the same way with Frank. He urges me to reach back into the crevices of my imprisoned mind while keeping me relaxed and calm. That day, he tries to help me remember what happened with Jared. But all I can recall is going with him for the day and running down the hallway far from him, terrified. Every session I leave exhausted, my nerves twitching. My mind is frayed like the memories are slowly eroding my sanity.

The memory of myself as a child running away from Jared crashes in on my daily consciousness, resurfacing at random times. I discuss all of it with Cliff while he listens attentively and tries to understand what I am going through.

"I don't know if it's real. Everything is so jumbled up inside my head," I say to him. "I don't even know if I'm real."

"I can assure you that you are very real." Cliff says decidedly. "Do these sessions help or make it worse?"

"I don't know. It's very confusing right now. Maybe I just need to push through it and see what happens. It might help me sort things out," I say, sighing at the mess in my head. "It's not like I have a lot of options."

"I have to believe this is going to help," I say. I don't want to be stuck inside my head. I want to move forward and choose to believe that Frank can help me do that. I need our boys to understand that problems can be solved, and when that happens, there is freedom, hope, confidence, and growth. I want them to be assured and to know who they are.

But the visions and memories keep me buried under a pyramid of emotions, that I cannot name. I question how long I can do this and if it will help. My confusion and shame lead me to cut my arms, in need of living proof of my very existence. I continue to question everything about myself and my life, constantly condemning my inner thoughts and images. I have no rest from my mother's condemning voice saying, "Shame on you!" I constantly analyze the stream of emotion that demands my attention. I worry that all my issues will stamp out the joy my children feel, and I work to cover up all the pain. I wish I had a manual that outlined the way to give my children a happy, hopeful life. I wonder if God loves me or if he is real.

I begin to contemplate the idea of reading my Bible. Just the Bible and no other church books. I wonder if it will lead me to the truth and peace I desperately seek. One night, after going to sleep, feeling the intensity of all my emotions, and crying out to God, I have a dream. I record it in my journal:

I see myself inside a deep and dark forest. I am surrounded by pine and cedar. The majesty of each tree looms over me like a thick carpet, shielding me from the sun and sky. Their heavy roots are sticking out starkly against the ground, leading me to guard every step I take. I feel afraid and trapped again. I find myself unable to move, but then I look up and there through a clearing in the sky I see large hands come down towards me. The hands reach me from the heavens, glowing and cutting through the darkness of the forest. I am filled with a peace that is intense and full, and I can't remember ever feeling it any other way. Colors that I've never seen before swirl around my feet as if it is prodding and pulling at me to release me from the tangled roots. I know immediately that God is reaching out to me. He scoops me up in his large hands, and I confidently rest against him. I feel his tenderness toward me. Then he transfers me to a place that is brighter and larger. It is an open space full of light and beauty. Wildflowers pop up from the ground spreading color around me and bringing me joy. I spread my arms out and start running in the large open field. Instantly, I am happy and at peace.

I wake in the morning with the dream vivid in my mind.

I feel a sense of hope and peace as I recall every slide like a movie in my mind. It feels like a sign from God. I believe he is telling me that he is there for me. He will show me the way. The hope blooms in my heart, even amidst all the dark and negative emotions. They persist. The darkness persists, but the bud of hope has been planted. When I discuss these feelings with Frank, he says that I am suffering from Complex Post-Traumatic Stress Syndrome, along with dissociative identity disorder and borderline personality disorder. I am taken aback by his diagnosis and feel he has just confirmed that I am crazy. I feel shame wash over me and vow to never tell anyone of this diagnosis. I immediately concern myself with the boys and instinctively pray for God's protection over them.

While my life at home can be overwhelming at times, especially with three young children, I still try to spend time with my friends and trade babysitting duties. My friend, Shari, and I trade meals because it saves us from cooking every night. Shari has two boys that are similar age as my two oldest, so they all play together well. Sometimes Shari and I visit and share about the day-to-day life with boys and husbands. She too grew up with Adventist beliefs. Similarly, my kids become best friends with Mildred's children. We often meet up to have coffee together. We spend our days discussing the doctrines of Adventism and question them. Mildred is a bubbly young woman with far out ideas. She pushes the limits in many ways and raises questions about why women should not wear bras and how Adventists know nothing about what the truth really is. I like her. She gives me hope that maybe all my questions do not isolate me but instead create community.

Cliff thrives at his work while enjoying life as a father and husband. I am always grateful that I get to spend my life with such a wonderful partner who is by my side through all the highs and lows of my life. However, it frustrates me that even his support and love cannot drive away the memories or visions. The images in my head are persistent, eating away at my consciousness. They leave me feeling empty to my core as if someone has scooped out my insides and left me hanging, hardly able to breathe.

Chapter 3

Months pass, and my therapy sessions with Frank continue. Memories tumble in and out of my mind like a tidal wave ready to envelop anyone in its path. One of the most vivid memories we explore was the murder of my brother when I was only 14 years old. He was my mother's first child. He was tall, dark, and handsome. He had a very charismatic personality.

The landline rings at my grandma's house late afternoon in August, and I answer. "Hello" I say hesitantly. I don't like to talk on the phone.

"Sharon this is Auntie. I'm going to be coming by to pick you up and take you home" She sounds weird.

"Okay," I'm not ready to go home, but she doesn't ask, and sounds determined.

I walk into our kitchen and see my mother sitting hunched over at the round table. Her face cupped in her hands, and she is weeping.

She looks up at me and loudly says "your brother has

been stabbed to death." I am frozen in the kitchen not sure what to think or do. My auntie consoles my mother, and my brother Shawn is motionless across from her.

I then blurt out "He's my favorite brother!" I turn and run upstairs to my room. I lay face down on the bed mulling over my words and condemning myself for being so stupid. How could I say something like that in front of Shawn? Why don't I just be quiet? What is wrong with me? My thoughts jumble into a ball and roll around in my head at a fast pace.

Shawn walks in my room and sits down on the bed beside me. He is five years older than me; he is the responsible one. He puts his hand on my back and gently assures me "it's okay, we all loved him, and we will all miss him." Shawn is tall with more of a lanky build than Bill. He has sandy blond hair and dark eyes. Bill and Shawn are half-brothers to each other and to me. My mother's first marriage is a secret to us at this point, then she married the father of my first and second brother, Joe and Bill. She always says that he is the only man she truly loved. She then married Shawn's father. Then my father. Then my stepfather. It feels like a lot.

I recall the memory to Frank; I notice that I feel afraid

he is going to tell me I'm being too emotional. Afterall, this happened years ago. More feelings pile up and I recall how I felt unseen, unheard, and unwanted after his death. "It should've been me, not him" I cried.

Frank sits beside me again on the couch and he reaches over and touches my back. "Did you cry very much after Bill died?" His hand gently rubs my back.

"No, I think I was numb. My mother was deeply grieved, and a lot of people came to comfort her. I felt like I needed to be quiet and stay strong. I remember the day after he died, I sat in the corner of the living room. I watched people filter in and out of the house, no one saw me."

Frank and I sit in silence, and then it's time to go. I feel comforted, seen, and heard by him. I imagine a loving father would be there for his daughter in the same way.

The days smoosh together like an old peanut butter sandwich, stale and sticky. Sleep is my only refuge during this time so being awaken by more bad news is not helpful. The phone rings with my grandfather urgently calling us to come to my grandmother's bedside. Upon arriving, I know it will be the last time for me to see her alive. She lay in her bed unable to speak. She's tries to tell my mother something, but the words will not come out. She looks afraid. She's rushed away in an ambulance as I stand in the yard, dazed by the past and present trauma. I want to ride with her to the hospital, but Joe pushes me out of the way and steps in beside her. He thinks he is her favorite; we all think that. She has a way of making each of us kids feel special. I feel more invisible during that time and force my feelings deep down inside of me. Only two days ago we learned that my brother was stabbed to death. It feels like all the people I love are leaving me.

I feel deeply troubled, alone, and distant from the life with her that I love. As I wait for news from the hospital I think of happy memories. My grandmother is a steady force of good in my life. I spend a lot of time with her, especially in the summer. She does not believe in the Adventist religion and considers my mother crazy because of her devoted love to Adventism. She is a rebel. She gives me coffee in my milk, something strictly forbidden by my mother. She feeds me bologna and white bread with sugar. She has cold cereal and pizza available when we stay with her, and Kool aide is her drink of choice. She loves to bake desserts such as cream puffs, chocolate cake, and cookies. She cans different foods such as tomatoes, beets, and green beans. She doesn't yell.

At Christmas she buys me a lot of gifts and then lets me open them early so she can buy new ones for under the tree! Yes, I love my grandmother, and life without her will feel lonely.

After she dies, people gather in our house to give their sympathies and condolences to my mother and us. But, again, I feel unnoticed and robotic. The thought of grieving is locked away as I tell myself to move on. People swarm around my mother and brothers, as I watch from the corner of the room. I am numb and will myself to pretend that I do not need comfort from others. I feel camouflaged as I lean against the wall alone inside my mind and my torment.

My therapy continues with the fast insult of one image after another. I work to put words to each one. In my session, I decide to talk about another memory that haunts me. Frank always sits on the couch beside me now, and I feel safe with him there. I don't notice that with each visit he moves closer, or he positions his arm differently. I focus on the memories and trust Frank with all the stuff that swarms my mind. "I remember driving to the airport with an older man named

Derek. He was someone from church. He was a shorter man with dark hair and black rimmed glasses. He drove an old pick-up truck, and I went with him to pick up a friend at the airport. It was about an hour away. When we arrive in the city, just outside the airport, he tells me that we can't go back the same evening. He said the snowstorm made it dangerous to travel, so he got us a hotel room. It was a room with two beds, and I remember crawling under the covers with my clothes on black pants and a silkie yellow blouse. I know what I was wearing because it was a birthday gift, I had just turned 16.

I felt tight and anxious inside as I hugged the pillow. I woke up the next day, with my clothes piled at the foot of the bed and no memory of what happened the previous night. But I felt shame crawling through my body, and I knew something had happened. My body was aching, and I felt like I was going to throw up. It was all a blank in my mind though, as I quietly snatched my clothes and dressed while Derek slept in the bed next to mine."

Frank listens and his hand gently caresses my long hair. "Do you want to look at this closer and see if you can remember what happened?" Frank asks.

I just nod and lay my head down in his lap. He begins to count, and my body relaxes. "You are safe now, Bethany. You can go back to that hotel room on that stormy night and remember what happened. You can tell me." His voice is deep and soothing.

My breath is steady, and I look through the peephole of my time. "Derek is Jan's boyfriend. Jan is the one we are picking up at the airport. They are both in their early thirties. At least I think we are picking up Jan, but we don't. She is not with us; we just go to the hotel room. It feels awkward. He says he doesn't need to call my mom because she already knows I won't be at home that night. For some reason I don't connect all the pieces. How can she know? If we are supposed to pick up Jan, why don't we go straight to the airport?" I begin to feel more distress as I start to see the bigger picture.

Frank reminds me that I am safe and directs me back to the hotel room. "Tell me what you see in the hotel room." He suggests.

"It's an older room. The beds have the usual hotel style bedspreads. The walls are a drab off-white with paneling on one wall. There's tan carpet." I look around the room for something interesting, but it's a boring room.

"Do you watch TV? Is it dark outside? Do you eat dinner?" Frank brings up some practical points.

"No, I don't think we do any of that. I do think it's dark outside, the curtains are drawn, they are brownish." I am silent for a few minutes, and I feel Frank touching my ear. "I think he just said it was time for bed, and then the next thing I remember is waking up with my clothes off."

"Did you have any dreams that night?" he inquires.

I begin to feel suffocated, like a pillow or something heavy is on me. I lose sight of my safe space and begin to wiggle as if I need to be free. "You are safe, Bethany. Can you tell me what is happening?"

"I think he is on top of me!" I move again. "I'm done now, please I am done." Frank begins to count the waves and tells me I can come back to his office. I sit up, exhausted.

The memories are like a volcano that continually erupts with destructive thoughts. We search for more in the deep recesses of my mind and unearth more unsettling visions. We talk about a sliver of a thought, another memory, and I tell Frank about how I went to church once with my mother.

"We are sitting in front of an elder. He is talking to a small group of people about something. I'm embarrassed sitting there and confused. I feel the need to hide, or at least look away. But I'm afraid of getting in trouble for not paying attention."

"What's going on?" Frank asks.

"He is standing in front of all of us and he's fondling himself while talking to us. I remember the look on his face as he keeps looking at me with a sly smile."

Again, Frank reassures me that I did nothing wrong. This man was an elder in the church, an adult, what he did was inappropriate.

The weeks creep by, and my therapy continues, leaving me in turmoil. Frank assures me that it is all quite normal and that it will get better with time. I choose to believe him. In between my sessions with Frank, I work to focus on Cliff and the boys, while painfully living with a volcano of memories that only get hotter.

The memories get more and more intense. With every snatch and vision, I question everything and wonder if anything I have known in my life is real and valid. Frank encourages me to put words to my emotions and memories. He wants me to focus on how it feels and find words to describe it. He tells me to believe the visions that bombard me. So, I try to do just that.

During sessions, I give in to his words and voice. I allow myself to relax and follow his lead. He counts, and I search for words to describe the images I see in my mind.

"Is this ever going to get better?" I ask him during one session.

"Yes. Keep telling me what you see and what's going on inside your mind. You are absolutely safe here," he says.

The images grow more and more intense. It scares me, and I am not always able to voice them.

"I don't know which of these memories are true," I confess to him. "I don't know where any of it is coming from."

"These are all memories that you repress. You separate yourself from them and categorize them with other parts of yourself. It's like you put them all in a drawer and locked it away, never to be opened again," he explains. "Now, try to remember what you were like as a little girl and let her out."

I imagine my childhood self in my mind's eye and think about her. Curious and sweet. My thick reddish-brown curls fall over one eye, hiding the hollowness inside. The smile on my face taunts the world with a masked fear.

"She wants her daddy," I whisper.

"Tell me more about that," Frank says as he lays his hand on mine reassuringly.

I find his touch to be comforting, like a father reaching to comfort his daughter. I imagine my dad to be like him. Maybe if he were more like Frank, he would have stayed with my mother and taken care of me. I spent years of my childhood looking for him. I searched in phone books for his name, and anywhere I can to find him. I asked my grandmother Rose, his mother, but she doesn't me anything. And then there he was, suddenly.

I find him right before Cliff and I marry. But he doesn't want to see me or have anything to do with me. I tell Frank all of this and the emotions bubble up inside of me. The pain of abandonment by my father, my lack of identity because he rejected my very existence, only confirms to me that I have no value.

"I felt invisible. I still feel like that. I was a girl without her father, and it made me feel empty. Every emotion, desire, thought, was sucked out of me. My friends all had their dads who had money, privilege and acknowledged their children. I felt like a girl that nobody could see. I believed I was invisible and irrelevant."

Heaviness fills the room as I reveal what I have been hiding, all that's bottled up since childhood. Frank wraps his arm over my shoulders and encourages me to rest against him. Exhausted, I give in to his comfort. But the darkness still lurks in my mind, and images flash through my head. I tell him about how, as I grew older, the need to belong only increased.

We discuss more memories that twist my insides with angst and dread. Frank asks me about my memories of being sexually abused. I tell him about another memory I recall.

"I went to my brother Joe's room. He tells me to get on his bed and forces me to perform oral sex. He pushes my head down, commanding me to open my mouth. And then he laughs. His laugh still echoes in my mind." I don't question this memory. It is etched with permanent marker, no, it's tattooed. Joe looks at me the same way that elder did the day in the church. A sly smile on his face as if he is undressing me.

I feel like a limp noodle by the time I get home from every session with Frank. Even though he comforts me, the memories, and the pain leave me feeling raw. It feels like I've been put through the wringer, and now I'm all tangled up and battered inside. It is not an easy feeling, and I am disgusted with my own memories. I question their validity, but I remember Frank's assurances. I scold myself again about being spoiled goods. I silently condemn myself to hell, believing that there's no way God will ever keep my name in the Book of Life after all that I've done.

"He says they are repressed memories. That the events of these memories are too much for my brain to handle at the time. As a defense mechanism, my mind represses all that can hurt me. According to him, I locked them away in a drawer and threw away the key. As they say, the human mind is a powerful thing. But now that I have opened the drawer; it feels like it is overflowing. I can't keep them locked away anymore. I think about closing the drawer again or finding a new place to keep them, but my power over them has diminished."

I lean against Cliff as we discuss the day's events. The boys have fallen asleep, and the house is quiet. Cliff listens to what I have to say and offers encouragement. "It makes sense to me that you would file all this away, how else would you survive?" Cliff muses. "This is a lot of stuff, no one should have to deal with this, especially a child!" His tone has touches of anger, and I am grateful he understands.

The next days, I watch the boys play and I feel inspired. I see them, and it gives me hope that I can move forward. I silently pray to God, asking Him to help me believe in His power and lead me to a place of knowing Him more. I write in my journal that He will show me He is real, and I will believe that I will know He exists.

I want the boys to know a God that always loves them, and I beg you God to show them. I believe they will learn if I learn to believe. But then, if God loves me, if he really is a good God, why would any of this be true? How could a loving Father allow such pain to a child? Where was He in all of this?

I show up at each session with Frank and try to work through the vivid screen of pictures that troll through my mind. I tell him about the memories of being pushed aside as a child. I was surrounded by affluent families when I grew up. My mother worked for such families. All my friends belonged to wealthy and influential people. I made friends with those children, but I never felt included. My feelings of loneliness and shame grew as if there was something wrong with me. I believed they pushed me aside because I wasn't good, smart, or pretty enough. I believed they laughed at me because I was ugly, fat, and boring.

I felt like I was on the outside looking in. Just on the sidelines, able to see and hear everything, but not invited to participate.

I felt minuscule and puny. I felt like the tiniest speck of dirt in the universe, worthless and nothing. I was living life as an outsider in a world of my own. I didn't talk to anyone about how I was feeling. I didn't think anyone could understand the complexity I felt inside. I continued to mask every feeling and hide them in crevices and corners within my mind, never realizing that someday they would all push to the surface.

With Frank's help, I continue to unearth memory after memory, the details swarming in and out of my mind. My life feels fragmented – like a shattered mirror. It feels like a jumble of puzzle pieces that I cannot assemble because I do not know what the whole picture looks like. If only I knew, maybe the despair that threatens me could lessen. I feel like I'm on repeat, continually mulling over the words that seem to describe the horrors that pass through my mind.

I pray to God and hope that my sessions with Frank work and bear fruit. I begin to write in my journal all that I hope to see in my future. I have continued to read the Bible and my discoveries are shocking. The God in the Bible loves me and calls me pure. He calls me a Saint and his grace has me covered. Yes, I have sinned, and I am saved by grace, but I am not a sinner. Sin does not identify who I am!

God says I am chosen. He says I am from a royal priesthood, a holy nation. He says that I belong to Him and that He will never leave or forsake me. He has called me out of darkness into His wonderful light. He says that I have received His mercy.

Oh God! Give me the ability to believe all that You say! Show me that you are real. Show me something!

Chapter 4

Everything I do is marked with therapy. I am not able to see a lot of progress in how I feel or where I'm going. With each session it feels like I'm drowning a little more as we drudge up the past and sort through the truth. My feelings are harsh and raw. I worry about the impact this is having on my boys. I have left the Adventist church and have not found a new place to attend. There isn't a community of believers that I feel comfortable in, so I continue with my own prayer and study. In fact, my Bible and prayer has become my main lifeline. Cliff is only half on board with leaving Adventism. He is interested in all that I'm learning and discovering, but he is also afraid that by leaving he is giving up salvation. We discuss the brainwashing that happens in this church environment, and I encourage him to simply focus on what Jesus has said. I am aware that my entire life I have been brainwashed. My beliefs about who God is and who I am are warped and because of this I must push through therapy and pray for the best.

"I'm not seeing positive changes in myself," I confide in Frank "What is wrong with me? How long will this take?"

"Therapy can take years," Frank says bluntly. "It took you years to get to this point. Now, you just need to work through it."

"I still struggle with what is true inside my head. If I don't know what's real, how can I work through it?" I ask him.

"You need more time. Maybe coming in twice a week will help you figure it out more?" Frank offers.

"But I can't afford that!" I complain.

"I'll give you a discount," he says. "The more you are able to put words to the memories that flash through your mind, the more you will see progress. As I told you, you just have them stored away deep inside your consciousness. Each memory has been carefully locked away in your brain, like a house with many rooms. When you can find the keys to each room, you will see and feel a difference. Why don't you tell me more about what you see when you go to your safe place?"

"I…want to. Progress, I mean. I'm not sure…" I mumble.

Frank moves to sit beside me and takes my hand in his gently, "You are very special, Bethany. I know it's hard, but I can help you. Do you want to go to your safe place now?"

I let my mind and body relax next to him as he starts to count. He starts describing the beach I always imagine, "The two of us are here on the beach now. You don't have to remember what you tell me in these sessions. We are just sitting on the beach together, and I am holding you close. You are safe."

I feel a quick check in my spirit at his words, but quickly dismiss the caution that I feel. Instead, I let my muscles loosen up, and I relax further on the couch.

"Let's go back to the man and the hallway. Do you remember what he looks like?" Franks says.

I sigh with weariness. I've never been able to remember more, and there is doubt lurking in my mind that I ever will.

I let the image replay in my mind. I see myself in a dark hallway where only a few beams of light are filtering through. I am standing at the end of the long hallway with a tall man.

"He has dark hair. He's tall and thin. He is supposed to be

showing me around his college campus, although I don't know why. I'm just a little girl," I tell Frank as the image sifts through my mind.

"Then what happens?" Frank asks.

"I ran away from him down the long hallway. I feel terrified. I don't remember why I feel like that. But I am afraid, and I want to get away," I can feel my clothes soaking through with sweat as my heart beats faster, and I want to resist the urge to run from Frank's office.

"You are safe, you are not there anymore. It's a memory," he reminds me comfortingly.

I try to calm myself down, reminding myself that I am not a child. I hang on tightly to Frank's arm and allow myself to believe in the safety he provides. Driving home, I can feel my mind turning, and my stomach churning. As each memory rolls in, one after another, I feel buried under their weight. Frank encourages me to put words to every image that flashes through my mind, but I feel strangled by them. I question their reality and my own reality. How does this help? I pray to God as I drive.

"Please show me the way! I've been doing this now for

what seems like forever, yet my mind is still racing in a circle of confusion and chaos. This is not who I want to be. I do not understand this. Please, God, just change me. If you are God, and You exist, please step in. Show me the truth."

"How was it today?" Cliff asks me as we do the dishes, and the boys make car noises on the floor in the next room.

"I don't know. Frank suggested I come in twice a week. Maybe it would help, but I don't know if the images in my head are real. I don't know how to put them into words. I feel safe in therapy, but I don't feel like it is helping. Frank said it could take years of therapy for any progress and that I have memories locked up deep inside my brain. Whenever I get scared, he holds my hand. It makes me wish for my dad," I honestly tell him my thoughts. "I mean it makes sense to me that this is a long process, and I've been storing it away somewhere in my head. It also feels so unreal, unless I start to see it, then it's terrifying to me. Then it feels real, but I tell myself I'm lying." I sigh in frustration.

"I'm glad you feel safe, at least. If anyone knows about timing, it will be him. He has a lot of experience, and I think pushing through it might be helpful," Cliff encourages.

With his words of support and encouragement, I set up appointments twice a week with Frank.

"We have two hours today," Frank says with a smile when I walk in and take my seat on the couch.

"Why? I thought it was 50 minutes?" I ask, confused. Thoughts of how much therapy is costing cross my mind.

"Well, I don't have anyone after you. So, we can use the extra time," he says nonchalantly. "Let's look at some other memories you have locked away. I will be with you the entire time."

He moves to sit next to me and slowly wraps his arm around me. I turn away from him slightly, feeling embarrassed, not knowing what to do or say. I often turn my back on him when working. I feel safer that way. I roll this around in my mind and wonder if it's normal for a therapist to sit close and wrap his arm around clients. It feels innocent, yet at the same time it leaves me with questions.

"It's okay. I am here to help you. Let's go to our safe place," Frank says.

Our safe place? I wonder. *I guess it makes sense that it's our safe place. When did it change from my safe place to ours?* He asks me to picture him there as well…

"We are on a white sand beach, and the waves are lapping over our toes gently," Frank starts to paint a picture of a sunny beach with the two of us relaxing on the white sand. "Now that we are safe, I want you to see yourself in my arms. I will keep you safe. As I hold you close, I want you to think about all the dark thoughts and images that come to your mind. Where are you? What is happening? How do you feel?"

Frank's tender voice urges me, and I start with caution, "I feel a lot of doubt about the images that roll through my mind. I wish I could better understand where they come from and if they are true."

"What do you see?" Frank asks.

"I am in the house that I grew up in. It is a small house, and we moved there when I was around eight years old, I think. My mother called a group of people from the church to come to our house. I think it's evening, and my mother is standing in front of me with her hands on my shoulders. 'I think you need prayer,' she says. 'I invited some church leaders to come and pray over you. Lay down on the couch'

She points to the velvet mustard-yellow couch. Our house is a cookie-cutter in a low-income neighborhood. It has an upstairs with four bedrooms and a bathroom, then a downstairs with the kitchen/dining, living room, laundry, and bathroom. For our family it's a big step up to be living in a house that is ours. It's the first house my mother purchased. The carpet is avocado green," I describe all the things I see.

"And do you lie down on the couch?" he asks.

I feel anxiety well up inside of me, and it becomes difficult to see myself on the beautiful beach with Frank. I can feel my heart racing, and my head begins to pound. I begin to squirm a little and wish I could escape.

"I need help!" I barely whisper

"What do you see? You can tell me. You're safe," Frank says.

"There are several people kneeling on the floor around me, their hands on me. They are loudly commanding the demons out of me. They want me to name the demons. They are holding me down!" I cry as tears stream down my face. "I don't know how to do what they are asking! One man tells me to repeat these names 'bad, liar, dirty, and pain,'" my voice trails off as I hear his voice in my head, commanding me to admit that I am full of demons.

Frank holds me tightly as I break down and cry on the couch in his office. I feel ashamed, confused, and scared.

"I am not sure what happened next," I sniffle as Frank keeps holding me, and eventually, my tears run dry.

"I talked about when my mother invited people over to pray for me, the time I was made to lie on the yellow couch," I tell Cliff the same night as we lay in bed. "I feel like I remember some of it, but at the same time, it doesn't feel believable to me. I think this happened on more than one occasion. Why would they think I had demons? What does that mean?"

Cliff hums and shifts closer to me.

"There are so many things that are causing me to question everything. I wonder if I am real or if I can determine what reality is." I muse.

"Does it really matter if it's real?" Cliff asks. "It's still in your head and causing you so many problems. It needs to be worked out."

"I guess that makes sense. I haven't thought of it that way before. I mean, how did all this get in my head in the first place?" I ponder this option "The longer I go on and don't see progress, the more I question the validity of it all. If God is real, then maybe he will change something for me, and I will see a way to overcome the haunting images."

My journal continues to be my processing place. I often go to the pages in my journals to write what is happening and sort out my thoughts and feelings.

I'm just not sure about the things I "remember" I still don't know where it all comes from or why I think what I think. He encourages me to say everything, but some of my thoughts are very dark. I feel like the life I thought I had as a child may not be the life I had. But how can I know for sure what is real? Does it matter? Will God show me the truth?

I am puzzled and flummoxed.

I close my journal after writing down my thoughts. I think about the day ahead. I love being a mother, especially with my boys. I'll be the first to admit that it has its challenging days, and I am often exhausted, but I still see them as a gift. I want them to have a happy carefree childhood. I want them

WHEN THE CHURCH THINKS YOU'RE CRAZY

to trust me and feel safe. I'm willing to do what I need to do to give them this.

My search for the truth and the need to know myself keeps me going to Frank twice a week. More often than not, our sessions go over the 50-minute time limit. He likes to point out that I am unique and different, and that he loves spending time with me.

"So, let's go back to some of your memories that include the people in church," Frank says as he sets his coffee down on the table beside the couch. Frank likes his coffee; he has a hot plate that he uses to keep his mug warm. I like the comforting smell of coffee in his office, and it reminds me of my grandmother. As an Adventist we were forbidden to drink coffee, but when I was with my grandmother, she always put a little bit of coffee in my milk. It was the best treat!

"I can try, but I'm not sure how much I know," I say meekly.

"Well, let's go to our safe place and talk about it there," he says as he scoots closer to me on the couch, his hip softly resting against mine. He takes me to the sandy beach inside my head again.

"There's an elder in our church who's with my mother, me, and a few others. He is talking to us about God and standing in front of where I'm sitting. As he talks to us, he fondles himself," I shiver at the images. "I feel flustered on the inside. I want to look or walk away, but I am afraid of getting in trouble. I don't know what to do because my mom is just sitting there, not doing anything. I decide just to sit there too, nervous about moving." This is a prominent man in the church, and I've had that image in my mind forever. I don't understand what was going on with him, but I do know it's uncomfortable. "There's so much more to this."

"Did anything else happen with that man?" Frank asks.

"He invited me into his office. I think I was between ten or twelve. I went in, and he closed the door behind us," I fall silent.

"Do you remember what happens after the door is closed?" he prods.

"No. I can see myself walking in, and as I turn around to look at him, he is closing the door. I get a feeling in my mouth when I talk about it. I feel like I am gagging. I have no recollection of what happens if anything, after he closes the door. I just know that when I think about it, I shiver and gag. My insides begin to feel all tangled up inside. I go from feeling like it was very bad, to telling myself that nothing happened. Then, I wonder why I have all these physical feelings too. I do remember his desk and the windows in his office had the blinds drawn. There were a couple other chairs in there for visitors." Exasperated, I put my head in my hands, wanting to extract the reality behind the memories.

Frank reaches out and caresses my back. His touch feels reassuring, but I feel a tingle inside of me at the same time. I sense a warning go off inside about Frank's motives, but then I dismiss it as stupid, silly, or just my imagination. Frank is helping me, right? He's a doctor, he knows how this all works way more than I do. If I can't trust Frank, who can I trust?

I'm feeling like I need Frank more than I should. He almost feels like an addiction to me sometimes. I don't know how normal this is, or what to do about it. It feels like I can't get better without his help, and yet at the same time, I will never get better with him…I need him. There's a check in my spirit that happens sometimes with Frank. I'm not sure what it means. But something doesn't feel right.

I dispel all my confused thoughts and emotions in my journal then file it away in the drawer.

"God, I don't know who you are or what you want. I don't know how to please you. Do you love me? I don't know the truth, but I do know that this is not freedom. Are you putting these thoughts in my mind, or am I evil? Please, help me see the truth. Help me. Do something that leads me to freedom and peace!" I pray silently, then pause.

I am not sure if God exists...

"If you exist, then please do something quickly. Or I will," I pray with determination, knowing that I am reaching my limit.

"So, how are you doing today?" Frank asks me as we settle together on the couch.

"Okay, I guess. I feel like I'm on repeat. I feel discouraged. Like I am not making or noticing progress still," I mumble as I stare at the carpeted floor of Frank's office. I look around at the bookcases against one wall and the desk snuggled in the corner. I notice the windows are up high and the curtains are drawn. I see that he has locked the door.

"You have been so brave and determined. I really love that about you," Frank soothes. "You have no idea how strong you are, Bethany."

"But I don't feel so strong. I feel exhausted, actually," I whine.

"Have more memories come up since we last saw each other?" he asks patiently.

"A couple, yeah," I admit.

He settles close to me and encourages me to move closer to him. It has become habitual for us to sit close on the couch. I usually have my back against him as he wraps an arm around me, holding me close. He starts with the visual and takes me to our safe place. I can feel myself relaxing instantly.

"We are together on the beach. It's just you and me, and we are holding each other close. We love each other," Frank says as he starts describing a story of us in love and together on the beach. "You can trust me. You can tell me everything that's on your mind, and I will help you feel better."

"Something doesn't feel right," I whisper.

"This is right for you. I am with you, and I will keep you safe. Now, tell me what you remember since you last came to see me," he says.

"I feel like I want to die. I don't notice any progress in myself or the peace that I hope for. I am still shrouded in darkness, and I feel hopeless," I respond to his urging. And then I pull out the memories hidden in the corners of my mind and start repeating the scroll of images that pace across my mind's eye, leaving behind the doubt, questions, and warnings that beat at my heart's door.

"Once, my mother took me to see someone that I do not remember meeting before. We go into a room with a massage table, desk, and some chairs. There's a nice smell in the room, I'm not sure what the scent is. I am not sure what he looks like, maybe he's tall and thin. He tells me to take off my clothes and lie on the massage table and then cover myself up with a sheet. The sheet is cold and crisp. I do not know what will happen, but I do as I am told. My mother doesn't say anything. She sits in the chair across from the massage table. The man touches me, and I space out, I think," I hug my knees.

I continue, "Then, I'm in the car with my mother, we are going home, we are in a mustard yellow Volvo that she bought from my uncle. I feel clamed up, my voice is gone and when I open my mouth to say something, nothing comes out. I'm dizzy, and by the time we are home, I am sick. I throw up. My body aches. I feel like a big truck ran over me and left me for dead. I am sick for days after that. I don't remember who that man is or his name. I don't remember what happens except that it felt horrible. I don't remember talking about it, and I don't think we ever went back."

"It's okay, you are doing very well," Frank grabs my shaking hands then starts massaging my shoulders gently. "You don't have to remember every detail. He shouldn't have touched you like that. You are so loved and special."

As he strokes my hair, I am comforted, at the same time, I notice the nagging feeling telling me to get out of there, get away from Frank! I convince myself that it must be a feeling that comes from memories. I feel silent pangs of shame wrapped up in heavenly comfort.

"Maybe it would help if you tell me about your dreams or fantasies," he muses. "I can tell you some of my own."

I sit silently, wondering what to say or do. I feel paralyzed by surprise at what he said. I wonder how this will help with the images in my mind or the dark thoughts that imprison me on the darkest of nights.

"I think about you during the week. Sometimes, I wish you would come to our sessions wearing pretty dresses so I could see more of you. It would be good for you to be more feminine and show off your body. God has given you a beautiful body, and I am someone you can trust with it. Every time I hold you, I want to be closer to you. I want to be with you, relying on God's grace to forgive any of my wrongdoings." he confesses. "Will you come next time in a dress? My dream is to see you in serene wrap and nothing else." He says with a hint of desire.

As if I couldn't be more surprised, he continues by telling me about a dream he had.

"I had a dream about us. We are in a beautiful hotel suite. You are wearing a white wedding dress; you look so beautiful. I'm in a tux, and I start to unzip your dress. But then I turn to look out the window and see a huge tidal wave coming towards us," he whispers in my ear. "Now, tell me you want to be with me too."

"I…do want to be with you. I don't know what to do without you. I don't know what else to say," I blurt out, the words twisting my insides. Questions are trapped inside my mind, and I begin to feel like a little girl that can't get away. What is happening right now? I wonder if I have done something to cause this turn of events. Is this happening or am I imagining this too? I really am crazy!

The pull I feel towards him is against everything I believe to be right and wrong. Yet, at the same time, I trust him. He is the doctor, not me. We pray during our sessions. He is also on the board of ethics and has been practicing for many years. I must be imagining things because it can't be real. He doesn't want to hurt me, does he?

"You can go to our safe place anytime you want, even if we are not together in my office. When you do go there, think about me being with you," he says, and his fingers play with my hair. "Will you wear a dress the next time you visit? I want you to think about bringing me pictures of yourself too."

I listen quietly, and I wonder how any of this will help me battle my demons. Then I rationalize that he is the one with the PHD, not me. He must have a method, and I should just trust him to do his job.

I leave Frank's office confused and full of questions. I'm torn about my trust and belief in Frank, I spend most of my time journaling. I write while the boys play outside in their treehouse. I love to sit outside on the deck and watch them run around in the yard and play. I desperately try to make sense of all that took place earlier in Frank's office. I tell myself that I've done something to bring this on and I just need to be more careful about the message I give him. I consider leaving therapy for a split second, but then I feel too afraid. I can't stop now that I have found a way to fight with my memories. I can't afford to lose Frank. *"Oh God! What am I going to do now?"* I whisper to myself.

Soon, my confusion turns to anger, which I project on Cliff. I feel frustrated because I don't know what to do. I want him to help me and get me out of the difficult position I am in. But all he does is listen and remain passive. It angers me, and I let it out sometimes. I feel ugly inside, and I take it out on him. I just wish there was a way for me to remain on this path without it getting so complicated. I feel sorry for myself as I think that everything I do, or touch turns bad. It would be better if I didn't exist, I'm just going to ruin Cliff and the boys' life. I am trapped.

***

The subsequent weeks tumble together in a jumble of thoughts and inner chaos. I do not know what to do with the mixture of pain and sadness. But there is also the fondness that blankets my thoughts for Frank. One bright sunny day, I leave the house in a flurry and drive to the coffee shop. I made plans to meet with two of my closest friends, Eleanor and Jocelyn. We have been meeting every week for some time now to study the New Testament and the life of Christ. I am learning and growing in my relationship with Jesus. But I still feel like I have a lot of questions about my life and Jesus. They have more wisdom than I do, and I know I can learn from them. I want to learn.

Our conversation takes off slowly as we discuss our children, work, and thoughts on the current study. Then the discussion deepens, and Jocelyn mentions that she and Eleanor have been going to a women's therapy group.

"The therapist that facilitates the group is an older woman," Jocelyn says. "Her name is Jane. She works in an office with another therapist named Frank."

I draw in a breath, letting it out with a shuddering exhale, "Is that Frank Smith?"

They both nod in unison.

"I haven't seen or met him but, I'm pretty sure that's the one. Why? Do you know him?" Eleanor asks.

"I do," I say. "I've been seeing him for about six years now. But I have doubts about it all now."

I fumble with the coffee mug, swirling the coffee inside.

"What are your doubts?" she asks.

"Frank comes highly recommended. I'm very consistent in seeing him. But now, I have doubts if that's a good idea for me," I feel unsure about what to say next.

"Well, therapy is hard. Do you feel like he is helping you?' Eleanor asks. "I mean, Jane is great for me. She helps me figure out some of the childhood stuff I struggle with. And she helps with our marriage too," she affirms.

Our conversation continues from that point as they both share their own therapy experiences. I can't help but notice how different it sounds from what I have experienced. They don't know much about Jane's personal life. She doesn't hold them close during sessions. And they only go for an hour once a week. I feel weird, and shame wells up inside of me. I feel sick for needing therapy as much as I do.

The next day, I settle down in Frank's office for another session. He tells me about another dream he had.

"I had a dream about us last night," he casually moves closer to me. "You are in a hotel room waiting for me. I come to be with you, and when you answer the door, you have a sexy gown on. I can't wait to touch you and be with you."

His hand rests on my leg.

"I don't know what to think about that," I crossed my leg away from him. "I'm married to Cliff. I love him and want to be with him. We have three amazing children together. That doesn't mean that you are not important to me, I have come to care for you deeply."

"It's just a dream. But I want to be with you, Bethany. I want to make love to you. I love you," he says, and I can feel the walls around my heart build back up. How did this happen? What have I done? The questions bombard me as I coat myself in shame and despair.

"Frank…I don't think I can continue seeing you anymore.

But I don't want to stop either. I don't know what to do. I feel that you are there for me, and I need that. It's hard for me to sort everything out. It's overwhelming. You are a steady listening ear." I tell him, feeling boxed in.

"We don't have to see each other in therapy anymore. We can meet outside. We can be together. I can meet you anywhere you ask me to," he says as if he deserves to have me. I toy with this idea as I feel very torn between leaving and staying. It's hard for me to imagine life without Frank.

His words ring in my ears, and conviction settles in my heart.

"I don't think I will come here again. It's hard for me to never see you again. I want to do what is right. I also want to be healthy, and this is not healthy." Silence rings between us as my words trail off - both of us deep in thought.

"We can continue to talk on the phone. Until it is the right time for us to meet again," Frank offers.

I stand up to leave and Frank gets up too. He stands close to me and reaches his hands out towards me. He puts both hands on my body and runs them down my sides. "I know this isn't normal." He whispers, "I just have so much fire inside of me and it is hard to resist you."

I leave his office. This is right. It doesn't matter, though, shame still finds a way to drown me. I am angry at myself for being in this situation in the first place.

What should I do? I wonder.

As Cliff and I sit together on the couch that same evening at home, I tell him about my decision and what Frank told me.

"I'm not going to see Frank anymore. He told me he had a dream about me in a hotel room waiting for him to come and be with me," I tell him and wait for his response.

Cliff just listens and simply comments, "Good idea."

The next day, I go to meet Eleanor and Jocelyn again for coffee. I wonder if they will bring up therapy once more.

"How's it going?" Eleanor asks me as we wait for our coffee.

"Okay, I need to talk to you about something. But it's confidential," I say.

"Okay," they both nod.

"I've decided not to see Frank anymore. He told me he

wants to see me outside of therapy. He had a dream about the two of us being together," I confess to my friends.

"Really? That is so wrong!" Eleanor coughs. "He has really crossed the line. Are you going to report him?"

"No. I didn't even think of that," I answer. "I feel embarrassed. And stupid. It's all a mistake. Frank is a good man, and I don't want him in trouble." I am quick to defend him.

"Did he just drop this on you, or has other stuff been happening?" Jocelyn says softly.

I don't respond. It feels like I've said enough, and I don't want to hurt anyone. I worry about what they might think of me. This is probably my fault anyway; I need to be quiet and hope it goes away.

That night, I sit down with my journal and tea, realizing that God has answered my prayer.

I asked for you to make things clear to me, and you have shown me that Frank's feelings are not healthy, nor are mine. I must remove myself from this relationship, somehow. This is so painful and hard. I have no idea how I'm going to move ahead. I do feel better about some things than I did when I started to see Frank, but now I feel like I have a new problem. What did I do to cause this? How can I know it's going to be okay?

A few days later, the house phone rang and brings me out of my reverie.

"Hello," I pick up the call, and he greets me simply,

"Hi," says Frank.

"Hi," I say.

"So, my coworker asked me about you. She threatened to report me to the board of ethics. I can't see you anymore. I don't know what you told her or what you think is going on between us, but you completely imagined it. None of it is real. You misinterpret everything! I am just trying to comfort you!" he says. "Why did you tell people lies about me? You know it isn't true."

His words snap something deep inside of me, and I see through the façade. I see the lies, manipulation, and the trap I have fallen into. I see that I am so desperate for help that I completely ignored all the warning signs. I want to believe that this will be helpful, so I blindly marched forward and allowed him to be inappropriate. I risked my marriage, my family, even my sanity for him!

"I did NOT imagine anything! Do not put things in my mind that are not true! I know what you said and how you touch me. I know how I feel," I yell at him. "You are a coward! You can't take all of this and throw it back on me. I come to you for help, and you betray my trust. You are a therapist! My God, how can you take advantage of a client and then blame the client?"

I hang up the phone and cry silently. I made the choice to end therapy, but to have Frank tell me that I imagine it all is ridiculous. The truth is very clear to me, and I have no intention of allowing him to tell me otherwise.

As I fall into a deep sleep, another dream fills me with hope. As soon as I wake up the next day, I write it all down in my journal.

I had a dream last night. I am standing in a large clearing. Trees are surrounding me. It's snowing. I look over at the trees and see Jesus walk into the clearing towards me. He is smiling at me. He's carrying beautiful boots, a red robe, and a warm fuzzy hat. He comes behind me and wraps me in the robe. He places the warm white hat on my head.

Then He walks in front of me and bent down to put fuzzy warm boots on my feet. He walks back behind me and wraps His arms around me. He says, "I am here with you. I will never leave you. I will comfort you, and warm you, do not be afraid. I am your reality and your truth."

I close the journal and make up my mind. I decide that I will pray about what to do next. Then I'll move forward from that point. I also confront my friends Eleanor and Jocelyn, asking them if they told anyone about what we discussed even though I said it is confidential. Jocelyn is the one who admits, albeit shyly, that she talked to her therapist, Jane, about the things I told them.

"I was really concerned," she says.

I glare at her, "Your therapist went to Frank and confronted him. Now, he's saying that I made it all up! I'm not going to continue living this way. I am not a victim. My life will have healthy relationships, and you are not one of them."

"Did you make it all up?" Eleanor asks me. "You really care for him and want to be with him, right? Why are you saying all these things about a professional therapist? I know he's on the ethics committee and doesn't do this to clients. He is well respected in the community."

"I did not 'make it up!' And yes, I do care for him. I thought he was safe, and I trusted him," I feel surprised, hurt, and angry by her question.

"Well, maybe you gave him the wrong impression," she responds.

"Do not make this harder than it already is. Maybe I did do something wrong, but that still does not excuse his actions!"

Tears well up in my eyes as I get up to leave. I feel awkward.

"I'm going to walk away because I love you, and I don't want to say any more. I think it's best we take a break." I turn to leave and say goodbye to friendships that mean so much.

The anguish in my heart seems to be never-ending. I want to forget about everything. I'm tired of hurting. I don't want to hurt Frank, but at the same time, I know I cannot hold all of this inside forever. I must move forward with a healthy change.

Which is why I find myself asking Cliff "I am not sure what to do next. I wonder if it will help to get some guidance from the pastor?" We are attending a new church that is non-denominational, and we both have a lot of respect for the pastor. "Do you think it's a good idea for us to talk to him? For some reason, I think he could guide us."

He agrees without hesitation, "Yeah, I think that's a great idea."

The next day, I make the phone call to Pastor Cooper's office and set up an appointment for the following day. He says he is willing to see us and talk. We drive to his office. He is a tall older man with thick gray hair who meets us at the door when we arrive. He proceeds to invite us into his office. He is an easy man to like. He leaves the door slightly cracked and turns to his desk to sit down.

"How can I help you both today?" he asks, folding his hands above the desk. His friendly smile immediately puts us both at ease.

"It feels good in this office," I say as I sit down in the chair across from his desk.

"That's the Spirit of God, He is present here," Pastor

Cooper says kindly.

I slowly begin to tell him about my therapy experience. I do not mention Frank's name, I'm cautious about saying too much. He listens intently, his eyes focused, and a sincere expression on his face.

"Cliff has just received a contract to work out of town, so I am overwhelmed with that, too. He is going to be in Pennsylvania. I feel stressed over the work I need to do and take care of the boys on my own once he leaves," I say as both Cliff and I chat with him.

"How are you coping with all this, Cliff?" the Pastor asks with sincere concern.

"It's hard to see her going through all this. I wish I had done something about it all sooner, but I trusted the therapist too. I didn't recognize what was happening, even though we talked about it. We want to believe that he had her best interests in mind and heart. I guess I was naïve. Now, I'm going to Pennsylvania for work but, she and the boys will be staying here, so I hate to leave," Cliff explains, remaining his usual calm self.

Pastor Cooper tells us that the boys and I should leave

with Cliff and get as much space as possible from the therapist. He also advises me to talk to an investigator about him. He even offers to have it all arranged. "This is something that never should happen." He stresses. "I believe you, Bethany, and in my opinion the healthiest thing for you to do right now is get some space with your family. God has a way of taking painful lives and making them new again. You are his child, he loves you, and he has plans for you. Jesus died for all of this, and you are not a victim. In fact, you are a thriver. Go to Pennsylvania and focus on the truth of who God is, this will change your life."

"That means a lot of change," Cliff muses out loud. "But I do think it's a good idea to speak to a detective about this, we can at least see what he has to say."

"I want to go with you." I tell him. "I'm willing to talk to the detective as well. At the same time, I don't want to make more trouble. I feel protective. I believe he is a good man, and he made a mistake."

"How do you know this hasn't happened before to someone else?" Pastor Cooper asks pointedly.

I am disheartened at the direction this has taken, but I also know it is the right thing to do.

I meet with Mr. Henley, the detective, a couple of days after our meeting with Pastor Cooper. He asks me a lot of questions about the time with Frank. I answer them honestly, feeling confident in what I remember.

"I feel like I want to protect him," I say.

"This needs to be reported to the State Board. His actions against you are wrong, ethically, and morally. He does not need protection. This is not your fault," he says.

His statement leaves me stunned, and I am scared because I don't know what will happen next.

God, I need you to guide me. Forgive me for the pain I cause, the poor choices I make. I know you promise to be with me, please show me more about who you are and who I am. Use me to be pleasing to you and to be the kind of mother my boys need. Thank you for bringing me this far, and for giving me glimpses of peace, I need peace.

Make a difference with your review.

"No one has ever become poor by giving" Anne Frank

Unlock the Power of Sharing

When we open our hearts and give without expecting anything in return, life becomes brighter and richer. That's the beauty of community.

Would you help someone like yourself—someone who's curious about faith, identity, and healing, but maybe a little unsure of where to begin or how to make sense of things?

My mission in writing When the Church Thinks You're Crazy is to offer understanding, hope, and a sense of identity to those who might feel lost, confused, or even trapped by ones they thought they could trust.

But to reach even more hearts, I need your help.

Most people find new books because of thoughtful reviews. That's why I'm reaching out to you to lend a hand to another seeker of faith, identity and healing, by leaving a review.

It costs nothing and takes only a moment, but your review could help…

- one more person find freedom on their faith journey,
- one more person find the courage to take difficult steps forward,
- one more person discover their path toward peace,
- one more person find a friend in these pages.

To make a difference, simply scan the QR code below and leave a review:

Leave Review

https://bethanyelle.com/amazonlaunch

If you love the idea of helping others, find their way, then we're kindred spirits. Thank you from the bottom of my heart.

Warmly,
Bethany Elle

Chapter 5

The opportunity to work in Pennsylvania doesn't come easily for Cliff. It's a result of losing his previous job. Cliff is very devoted and committed to his career, our kids, and me. He loves his work, but his priority is his family. The company he worked for refuses to acknowledge that he needs at least one day off per week. Cliff won't do that; he wants to spend at least one day at home playing with the kids and spending time with me. So, when he does not submit to their demands, he was fired for wanting to spend too much time with his family.

I step into our bedroom to find Cliff sitting in the chair by the window. He is somber. I sit on his lap "How are doing?" I ask.

"Not the best, I'm stressed." He sighs. "It doesn't feel good to be fired."

I lay my head on his shoulder "I'm so sorry."

He begins to cry as we sit together in our bedroom, the morning sun peeks through the window. I can see the leaves from the willow tree sway in the breeze and I feel God is with us. "God will bring you to a stronger and better place. He loves you, although it doesn't always feel that way. He loves our boys, and he will take care of us. I think being fired for the reason they gave is noble."

"I know I can find work; it's just that there is so much travel involved. I think Pastor Cooper is right, we all need to go." His voice is resolute, and he breathes in deeply. "I will go first; you and the boys can stay here and get things packed up in the house and settled. Then, in few weeks I'll fly home, and we will all drive to Pennsylvania."

Cliff's decision to start his own company as a consultant is one of his best. He has a lot of experience and has his fair share of contacts. Not only does he have work in Pennsylvania, but several big-name companies hire him for consulting work. The job in Pennsylvania is with a publishing company and he consults with them on technical matters. We are approaching the year 2000, and there is a lot of hype about what will happen to the computers and the world in general. His job is to assure them that when the year turns over, all things run well.

After our decision, per Pastor Cooper's advice, to move

to Pennsylvania, we carry out the plan busily wrapping up details in our hometown as we prepare for the long road trip. We plan to put a lot of our things in storage and only take a small amount with us. I instruct the boys that they are each allowed two boxes to take with them, the rest we must leave until we return. The idea of driving across the country to a new place is exciting to them. We rent a car dolly so we can pull a car behind us packed with belongings and then pile into our SUV for a big adventure. Upon arrival we move into an apartment that Cliff has found for us and begin a new phase of healing.

Amid all this my friend Mildred introduces another fun adventure. She asks me to travel to Europe for two weeks on vacation with her sister, Ingrid, as well as her friends, Liz and Janet. I decide to say yes because I believe it will be an excellent way to get away from all the stress and the situation with Frank. "I have decided to go with you all to Europe" I announce one day as Mildred and I have coffee. "I don't have a good backpack for the trip. Where did you get yours?" I inquire.

Mildred is excited that I will be joining the group. I don't know her sister very well and I've never met Janet or Liz.

"This is going to be so much fun! I can't wait." Mildred says excitedly. "If you check out the backpacks at REI you will likely find something that works for a two-week backpacking trip" No one in the group has been to Europe before and none of us have lived out of a backpack for two weeks! This will be an adventure.

I meet the group at the airport. There's a lot of excitement and anticipation. I am the only one in the group that has flown internationally.   I sit with Janet and Liz on the flight. They are both in their thirties. Liz is married, Janet is single. Liz has something to say about everything and keeps us laughing with her funny antics. Janet is quieter and mild mannered. The three of us connect right away and feel like the best of friends by the time we touch down in London. We plan to spend a couple days in London, then take the Eurostar to France. After a few days into our trip, we sometimes break off into two groups due to different likes and dislikes. Mildred goes with her sister while Liz, Janet, and I explore on our own.

Mildred and Ingrid plan to stay in hostels for most of the trip, but the rest of us have other ideas. "I'd rather stay in a nicer hotel," Janet comments one day. "Does anyone want to stay with me?"

"I will!" Liz says enthusiastically.

"I'd like that too," I agree, imagining a comfier bed and more privacy.

"You ladies are like pampered poodles," Mildred says sarcastically. "All you want to do is stay in hotels, shop, and eat at different restaurants." I notice that she disapproves.

Janet, Liz, and I enjoy a comfortable evening in a hotel room in Paris. We watch the movie Pretty Woman all in French and offer our own interpretation as the movie moves along. We have a lot of fun.

On one of our Paris days, we walk into a salon in hopes of a chic haircut. Janet decides it's too adventurous for her and she watches as Liz and I point to our hair and pictures in hopes that the French speaking women will understand. Two hours later Liz leaves with curly layers and I with a Pixie cut. We both love our hair and can't wait for another mysterious adventure.

Days into our trip, while we are traveling from one country to another on the train, Mildred suggests we tell each other stories about our lives to get to know each other on a deeper level.

"We've been together for a while now, and we are all getting to know each other," Mildred comments as we settle on the train that will take us to Germany. "For instance, I've known Bethany for years, but there is still so much about her I don't know. Let's tell each other our stories!"

One by one, each one of them shares their experiences and stories that are full of ups and downs. They share their experiences of accepting God into their lives and living a life for Him.

"What about you, Bethany? What's your story?" Mildred asks.

At first, I don't know what to say; it's challenging to think beyond the last few years. The last few months have many new changes for me. Most nights, I cry myself to sleep because of the emotional turmoil I feel. I feel weak and vulnerable. I pray to God, asking Him to bring me clarity and peace, as well as wisdom on dealing with Frank. I feel like I need to protect Frank's identity, but at the same time, I feel like I betrayed Cliff even though he never said that. So, I draw in a breath and start with what comes more comfortable to me.

"I'm married with three sweet boys. I'm a stay-at-home Mom with aspirations to write a book someday. I've homeschooled the boys for a couple of years, but now they will be going to a private school. We are in the process of moving to Pennsylvania for work. I'm excited to see what that will be like. I'm still getting to know God on a deeper intimate level. I grew up in a restrictive environment, so leaning into God and trusting him is still new for me. I have a lot of changes in my life right now, and questions. I can see how He answers some of my most desperate prayers. I see how He is guides me through difficult times," I pause as unwanted tears well up in my eyes.

"It's okay, Bethany. We're here for you," Liz comforts me, gently touching my shoulder. "Moving is stressful, and combined with travel, kids, and other changes; you have a lot going on!"

I like these women, but I am not comfortable divulging everything about myself. I measure my words carefully as I continue.

"I started therapy due to some childhood stuff I was

dealing with. The therapist is a good, educated Christian man. I like him and trusted him. As therapy continued, some lines got crossed, and I felt confused most of the time," I tell them.

Janet leans forward with compassionate interest, "That sounds tough. I also see a therapist. His name is Dr. Frank, and I know just how important it is to feel safe with your therapist. If the professional lines are crossed it can really mess with someone. I'm glad you are not seeing him anymore."

My heart stutters at her statement. "How long have you been in therapy? Do you find it helpful? Where does he practice?"

"I've been going about a year." She begins "It is very helpful. Frank is great! I feel safe with him, and I trust him with some of those childhood secrets. He is right in town so it's close to my house. He has another therapist in there with him, a woman. I think her name is Jane, she does groups. I'm thinking about joining one of her groups." Janet easily explains her therapy experience.

"I've heard of a Frank Smith, is that who you see? I've

heard he is on the ethics committee too." I casually ask and to my absolute horror, she confirms that her therapist is indeed Frank Smith.

That evening I feel the world is closing in on me. There is a heavy cloud hanging over this amazing vacation, but the struggle to enjoy it is prevalent. I pull out my journal tucked away in the bottom of my pack and begin to sort out my feelings on paper.

I'm so, so ready to be home. This is a wonderful trip but finding out that Janet sees Frank is tough. She's talks about her relationship with him and how special he is. I am not sure what to do. Do I tell her of my experience with him? Do I ignore this?

As I put my journal back in my backpack, Mildred walks through the door. She sits down beside me with a sigh and asks me the question I was dreading, "Did you see the same therapist as Janet?" Mildred knows that I had a negative experience with my therapist, and I talked to a detective. She doesn't know how intense it is or any of the details.

"Yes," I answer.

"What are you going to do?" she asks.

"I don't know," I respond, wanting to protect everyone involved.

In the next couple of days, we settle down in the train after putting our backpacks away, on our way to Italy now.

Ingrid shoots me a skeptical look and says, "Did you ever cross the line with him? It's just that I've been thinking about what you said, and I wonder what *you* did to provoke him?" She crosses her legs and purses her lips. Her red hair is tangled from days of travel, and she looks tired.

"I make mistakes, too. I stayed in therapy too long, and I trusted him way too much," I confess.

"Does anyone else have a similar experience with him?" she asks with an inquisitive expression.

"I have no idea," I admit honestly.

Ingrid's questions stir up more turmoil in me. I ask myself and God the same questions as I stew in guilt and shame over my own lack of discernment. We fall silent and retreat to our private thoughts.

I feel such anguish deep within my heart. I feel so hurt and betrayed. I care for Frank, yet I see that he takes my difficulties in understanding what memories are real and uses it to try to convince me that what he did is not real. He is manipulating me and using his power as a professional to keep me quiet. I know better! I know what he said and where he sat in our sessions. I know that he touched me. I remember every detail he divulged about his personal life. I wrote everything down, which helps. He is afraid of being found out because he knows what he is doing is wrong. My friends, or so-called friends, want to blame me, but I will not accept the blame. I will work towards living the truth, fully and completely. I will not be manipulated anymore!

God, show me what to do. Forgive me for the part I have in this. I know you guide me, please show me who you are and who I am. Use me to be pleasing to you and to be the kind of mother my children need. Please bring the truth out about Frank and give me the strength to deal with it.

After the trip ended, Cliff and the boys greet me at the airport. I grab my boys and hug them tightly, so happy to be home. The boys have not seen their friend Ben, Mildred's son, while I was traveling. Now, they are excited to meet up with him before we leave for Pennsylvania. A few days later, I meet with Mildred, and we sit down for coffee together in her kitchen. Meanwhile, the boys continue to play in the backyard.

"Ingrid and I went to Janet's house yesterday. We told her that the therapist she is seeing is the same one you saw." Mildred tells me.

"What? Why would you do that? It wasn't your place!" I lament, shocked that they would break my trust like that.

"Well, she doesn't believe it anyway," Mildred snorts. "She said there is no way Frank would be inappropriate with a client. He's on the ethics committee, for God's sake!"

"I wish that were true. But he is inappropriate with me, and that doesn't change just because you or Janet refuse to believe me. I believed he was safe, but I am mistaken." I respond firmly.

"But do you think you led him to believe it was okay?" she asks, sipping her coffee. "You don't exactly have the best social skills. In fact, you are socially retarded. I think you misinterpret what is going on."

"I did not misinterpret anything!" I say through clenched teeth, visibly angry. I get up from the kitchen chair and call my boys, "Come on, boys! We have to go."

I gather them, and we walk out the door.

Then, Mildred calls me a week later, "We don't think it's a good idea for the boys to play together anymore. We don't trust the influence Ben will be exposed to."

The loss and hurt build up deep inside me for weeks afterward. I wish I had not said anything to the ladies while traveling. I feel sad that I have lost more friendships and chastise myself for trusting them. I am sad that the four traveling companions do not believe me about Frank. I question the reality of friendship with Mildred in the first place. Cliff, being the compassionate and level-headed man that he is, tries to talk to Mildred and her husband, Harold. But they have made their decision, and it is final. And so, I place another friendship on the back burner, determined to move on with what I know to be true about my own life.

"I feel so horrible! Due to my actions and stupidity, our boys are separated from one of their best friends," I cry to Cliff. "Why did I say anything? What is wrong with me?"

Tears overflow as I process the phone call from Mildred. I don't know how to break the news to the boys. I have no idea what to do!

"Mildred and Harold have decided to take a break from our friendship, which means we won't be seeing Ben for a while," I slowly begin to explain the messy situation to our boys without going into details. "We will be living in Pennsylvania soon anyway so we can hope things change when we return."

And so, we start our journey across the country in our truck pulling our small white car behind us.

"How long are we going to drive?" The boys ask excitedly. "Are we almost there?"

I glance at Cliff and see a smirk flicker across his face at their excitement.

"We have a long way to go. It's going to take three days before we get there. This is going to be a very long drive!" Cliff answers.

I smile because I know we will hear the same question every couple of hours. I wonder how many stops we'll see before we arrive at our destination.

I feel the tension leave my body as we trek further East. I have a lot to process, and I am grateful for the opportunity to start again and have time to think. "I feel good about this." I say out loud.

The boys settle down for the long day and play games like the alphabet game, and I spy. They make funny signs and tape them to the back window. We listen to music and stories.

We drive through mountain passes, open prairies, and some deserts. The whole journey is a beautiful and exciting experience. Cliff and I chat back and forth about the scenery and the past few weeks.

"I'm thankful we are with you," I tell him. "This is going to be good for us as a family, and it feels good to get some distance for me. Thanks for not giving up on me through all this."

The smile remains on my face as we converse. It is true. Cliff is the backbone of my life. He is kind, loving, and patient. He wants me to feel better.

"I'm relieved that you are out of Frank's office. We trusted his methods, and that was wrong. I believed he knew what was best, but I should've intervened somehow," Cliff confessed. "I was naïve."

"We both were. You didn't know," I reassure him.

Guilt and shame eat me up for the conflicting feelings that surface for Frank. I know Cliff is the love of my life, and I can trust him with anything, even my life. I am utterly grateful for the solidarity and loyalty he shows me and the strength he has mustered to walk through this situation with me.

"I wish I hadn't said anything to Jocelyn and Eleanor," I say, my voice cracking with emotion. "Now they don't want anything to do with me and think that I seduced Frank! All the people I thought were my friends think I'm a liar and a seducer. I'm not sure trusting and being vulnerable to that degree is a good idea, after all."

"You are being honest about your experience. It's too much for them to handle. This is not about you trusting too much; it's about their inability to walk through pain with a friend. There will come a time when you find better and safer friends. At the same time, it is because of Jocelyn that this worked out in your favor. If Jocelyn hadn't said anything, Frank wouldn't be scared."

His words prompt me to write in my journal:

I feel safer now that we are far away from Frank. God, I

know I make so many mistakes. Please keep my children safe and healthy. I do not want to see their lives messed up because I take so long to figure everything out. Show me your truth. Open my eyes to the way You desire me to go. I leave all of this in Your hands. I know that You want the best for me. I have not heard anything back from the investigator that I spoke to. It feels like it will somehow all be pushed away and never discussed. I will do whatever it is You decide for my life. Just give me Your strength and wisdom. I need You. My experience with people is a continual pattern of loss, show me how I can change this. If there is a reason for all of this, help me to understand! Change me to be like You. It takes me a long time to believe that You are good. Now that I see your interventions, show me how to turn my despair into hope and love. I want to live in Your truth and bring Light to others.

Chapter 6

Our move to Pennsylvania is good from the start. The boys are excited to live in a new place and have new bedrooms. We rent an apartment on the second floor of a large complex across from a beautiful park. We have plenty of room to meet our needs, and we all love walking and playing in the park. We also have a huge grocery store on the other side of the complex and it offers anything our hearts desire. On weekends, we go to New York City, or Atlantic City. We expose the boys to Phantom of the Opera on Broadway, Central Park, and New York pretzels. We visit Philadelphia and Washington D.C. browsing through museums and tasting new food from street vendors. Everything is fun. I am pleased that the boys get to have all these experiences and learn so much.

We have friends visit for a week and I take them to New York. We buy bags of jellybeans and visit the World Trade Center. It feels good to have friends that want to be with us.

I feel more at peace; the images in my mind are less frequent. I credit this to God, and the time I spend with him.

I talk to God every day he is my best friend. I concur that he knows everything about me, so I may as well talk to him about every detail. I am not rejected by him or condemned. My thoughts about life change, and I feel at peace. When the images and flashbacks do invade my mind, I remind myself that it is not a present concern. I learn to replace the negative images and thoughts with the truth of my present life, as the truth I am learning about God and myself.

I have decided that whether the images are real or not, I will confront all the misery and torment. I must face it head-on, along with the truth that God gives me in His word. I focus on studying identity. Who is God? What does He think of me? Who does He think I am? And are my thoughts aligned with His thoughts? The more I change my thought patterns, the more I believe in God's promises. I soak in His presence and tangibly feel His peace healing me. I learn about the Holy Spirit and see that when I lean into the presence of God and his Spirit, I discover God's thoughts.

And just like that, eighteen months pass by, and our time on the East Coast comes to an end. Cliff's work contract finishes, and we are free to live wherever we want. We decide to leave the choice up to our boys and ask them where they want to go. They tell us they would love to live just a few miles south of where we were before. Cliff stays behind with the boys to pack up our things while I fly West to look for a new house for us to live.

I find a quaint little white house right downtown. It needs work, but the price is great. I make an offer and quicker than we expect the house is ours. I hire a contractor to remodel the house and ask a friend to oversee the details while I fly back to Pennsylvania to finish up last minute packing and then drive with two of the boys to our new home. Cliff and our oldest son wait a couple more weeks to wrap up last minute details, then they drive the moving truck across the country to our new home.

On our way to our new home, we stop to stay with a dear friend. She is a mother figure to me and has been in my life for years. She has agreed to continue the drive with us and see our new house. I am excited to be with her. I met her when I was 15 years old, and I left home to go to boarding school. I'm anxious and don't know exactly what I am getting into. It's my first time away from home, and everything is strange and foreign to me. I notice that I am very different than the other kids at the school. I eat differently, dress differently, and process differently. I am weird. Lucy oversees all the girls, and she can see that I need someone to love me. She immediately takes me under her wing and helps me learn the ropes. She teaches me what all the ringing bells are for, which rooms to go to for classes, and how to socialize. She sits with me and helps me understand the day-to-day routines, and she prays with me. She loves me. I spent all my high school years at this school. I do four years of schooling in three years, and I leave there knowing that Lucy will be in my life forever. She is not fazed by anything I tell her; she tells me she loves me, and she commits to being my Heart-Mom for the rest of the days she lives on earth. She is exactly what I need.

Lucy is not the only one that speaks into my life in those formative years. My English teacher, Callie, inspires me to be a better person. She gives her time, love, and understanding to me. She teaches me to play the piano, improve my writing, and not to be afraid. Callie can see the pain in my heart.

On our wedding day, both Lucy and Callie are there. As I walk down the aisle, excited to begin a new chapter in my life, Callie plays a beautiful melody on her flute. I am still in touch with Callie to this day and will not forget her positive influence on my life. I am grateful.

We settle into our new home and the boys make friends right away with the neighbors. Then, I get a phone call that puts things in motion.

"Hi," an unknown woman on the other end says. "Is Bethany available?"

"Yeah, hi. This is Bethany," I answer, wondering who it is.

"My name is Madeline. I am a lawyer for the State, and I've been reviewing your case," she responds.

"My case?" I ask, confused.

"Yes, your case with Dr. Frank Smith. Are you available to meet with me and discuss it?" she asks me.

"What do you want to know?" I say flatly.

"Well, Dr. Smith crossed many boundaries in your therapy sessions. We want to file a lawsuit against him and see if we can compensate you for any damages incurred," she explains clearly.

"Oh. I can meet with you if that will help."

Before ending the call, we set a date that works for both of us and mark it down in our calendars. I make the drive to a nearby city for the meeting. At first, I don't want to do this at all. I want things to go back to normal and to go away on their own. I want to go back to Pennsylvania where everything goes smooth. I don't want to lose the peace I am feeling or any progress I have made so far. As I drive, I can feel the familiar shame, sadness, anger, and fear knocking at my heart. I feel anxiety over what might happen, and I find myself recalling events with Frank as we sat together on his couch.

I meet with Madeline, a 35-year-old woman. She has sandy brown hair, curled into a stylish bob, framing her soft features. She has a deep voice and is very welcoming. I immediately feel comfortable thanks to her warmth. She has invited a co-worker that has more experience in cases like mine and we all sit down together.

As the meeting starts, she tells me that she wants me to know that what happened with Frank is not my fault. She stresses that he is a predator and is emotionally manipulating me. She says that he groomed me to fall into a trap, and with my history I couldn't have seen it coming. She also tells me that she is confident she can win this case. She thinks he deserves to be reprimanded for what happened and says that all I need to do is tell the truth. I am clear on what the truth is, and I too am confident in my ability to do as she asks, so I agree to follow through with the case.

She proceeds to ask me for more details, and I tell her everything. I tell her about the painful flashbacks that race through my mind and how they confuse me so much that I went to seek help from Frank. We talk about the painful decision to leave therapy and how he wanted to meet outside of therapy. I painfully recall the fantasies he shared with me. And the disquietude they left me in.

"He gave you three diagnoses, CPTSD, DID, and BPD. Do you agree with that?"

"I don't know. I do think the complex post-traumatic stress disorder is correct. I question the dissociative identity disorder and the borderline personality disorder. Having said that, I believed he knew more than me concerning these things and behaved accordingly. In some ways, I think I wanted to be who he said I was because I didn't think I could figure it out myself. I have read up on all these disorders and the CPTSD is the most fitting." I muse.

I remember how he prompted me to dress more provocatively and how he gradually got closer to me during our sessions under the guise of comfort. I admit how I cared deeply for him and sometimes questioned if I should be with him. I cry over the control I allowed him to have over me, feeling shame and pain over my stupid actions.

I anguish over the conversations I had with Mildred and the others that I traveled with. I admit how their accusations only made it more challenging for me to sort out what was true. The meeting closes after several hours. They're both very kind and honest with me about next steps and my involvement.

"We assure you that after talking with you, we will win the case and fight for you to get refunded every penny, among other things," Madeline sat her pen down on the wooden table and looks me squarely in the eyes. "Do you need time to think about it?"

"No, I will cooperate," I respond decisively. I feel a peaceful resolve and a deep conviction that I'm doing the right thing. It will not be easy. I will likely feel afraid and maybe want to quit, but I must do this!

Madeline tells me she'll get back in touch with me and asks me to gather my writings during the time I spent with Frank that has any reference to Frank or any other evidence I have of my relationship with him. I think about all the years with him and the many journals full of information. I tell her that I have years of information, and she assures me the more the better. I wonder if he too will give information, such as pictures he has of me, letters I wrote, and possibly recordings.

A couple weeks later, I process the situation with Cliff.

"I have a deposition in four weeks. Madeline called today and gave me the news. She said that Frank has hired a lawyer from San Francisco to fly over for the deposition. She also told me to be prepared for a rough day," I tell him. She warned me that his lawyer is tough, and most people crumble from his interrogations.

Madeline calls earlier in the day. She assures me we will win the case because of all the evidence we have against him. She warns me to be ready for all the tough questions from Frank's lawyer.

"I wish I could be there too," Cliff says, sounding

regretful. "You can do this. You are the strongest person I know. It's all going to work out."

His confidence gives me faith that things will work out. Madeline meets with me a few days before the deposition to go over the details once again.

"Wear comfortable business casual clothes," she explains. "We might be there for several hours, so you want to be comfortable."

Before the deposition, I have feelings of guilt for reporting Frank. I feel scared and nervous that nobody will believe me. I pick up my journal to write out my prayers to God and process my doubts, fears, and anguish.

God - You say that you are Sovereign. You tell me that You love me and that you will never forsake me. You cherish me and tell me that I am the apple of Your eye. You are my Defender! You promise to fight for me, give me the ability to surrender to You, come what may. Forgive me for not trusting and believing You or not seeing that you have a plan. I don't think I can do this. I'm too afraid. How am I going to sit in front of Frank now? How am I going to find the words to describe how it was, how it feels? How will I do this?

The deposition is a couple days away, and I fret over what to wear. Madeline has told me to dress "business casual," but I am a jeans and t-shirt gal! So, I go to Nordstrom and browse for hours. I settle on grey capris, a white sweater, and simple black heels. The morning of the deposition, I stop to get an Americano at Starbucks, the hot coffee instantly settles my nerves, and I ease into the seat of my old Land Rover.

I start to pray, *Oh God, I am afraid! What if I can't do this? What if I freeze when I see Frank sitting there? What if I can't remember what happened? I wish this would all go away! Holy Spirit rest upon me and give me your words and your memory, for you never forget anything and you know what to say. Keep my emotions intact so I am steady. Hold every emotion and thought in your hands.*

I spot Madeline waiting for me outside the office building. I park my Rover and walk towards her. She tells me Frank and his lawyer are already inside the room.

"We will sit across from them, and his lawyer will ask you questions," she informs me.

As we walk inside, I see a smirk across Frank's face. We

take our place across from them. As I sit down, I whisper a prayer to God to lead me in truth and clarity. I remind myself for the umpteenth time that Jesus is my reality, and as long as I focus on His truth, I will be okay.

Frank's lawyer starts, and he is relatively gentle in the beginning. He starts with simple questions and a gentle voice. As the day progresses, his questioning becomes more intense.

"You are the one that seduced Mr. Smith, isn't that correct?" he slams his hand on the table and stares at me with sharp blue eyes. "You are the one who is confused about reality and imagine all kinds of dark things in your mind, am I not correct?"

"You are not correct. I did not seduce Frank. I trusted and believed him. And yes, I struggled with the images in my mind and questioned their reality," I hold my own boldly, not letting him bully me into admitting to things I had not done.

"How can we believe anything you say when you are the one that is out of touch with reality?" he does not take his piercing stare away. "You say that Frank sat next to you and held you during your sessions. Did he ever hurt you? Was he comforting? How do we know you didn't imagine him sitting there?" His face is close to mine, as he sharply interrogates me.

I refuse to flinch away from his accusing words even as he puts his face close to mine. He continues hurling questions at me.

"You told your attorney that Frank revealed personal and intimate details about himself and his family. What did he tell you?"

"He told me about his children, his wife, his dog. He mentioned the artwork on his walls, and where he lives. He said he thinks about me while having sex with his wife. He said he has a lot of passion and fire, and he wants to make love to me. He told me all about his hobbies." I continue with the long list of information I have about Frank.

Franks lawyer bombards me with more questions, but the Spirit of God buzzing in me. My thoughts remain lucid, and I hear him whisper to me, *"I am real, Bethany. I will guide you and give you all the right words. My Spirit is alive in you; my grace is upon you. I will not leave you, not ever! My peace is with you, and you are victorious."*

I know I need to focus on Him. He will give me the strength and the ability to voice out the truth boldly. Frank's lawyer hurls his questions at me for 12 straight hours. He drills me about every detail of my time with Frank and reads excerpts from my journal that I submitted. His voice rises with each question and his face contorts with tense emotion. Throughout it all, Frank sits quietly, sometimes he shakes his head and other times looks at me with pity in his eyes. He never speaks unless asked. I realize that his lawyer wants to break me. He wants me to cry hysterically or curl up in a ball of despair. His anger only intensifies as he fails to accomplish my demise.

Meanwhile, I confidently answer every question thrown at me, emboldened by the supernatural strength and clarity I sense inside of me. I find am grateful for the current moment because it enables me to witness the power of God within me.

After the deposition is done, I go home, I hug my boys and Cliff, then curl up in bed and sleep the burden away.

"It was super hard and invigorating at the same time," I

confess, as I soak in the tub full of hot water, and Cliff listens. "I feel like I went through therapy all over again. I feel stripped naked – bare and vulnerable. I also feel empowered, supported, and clear. I think Frank and his lawyer are afraid because they know he is in the wrong. I'm not going to be his victim!"

"You did it! Now, they will decide whether to go to court or to settle. He knows he's guilty. Why else would he hire such a hotshot of a lawyer? He knows he can't win this. They will settle, and it will all be over soon," Cliff says confidently.

***

Weeks go by, and we settle deeper into our house. But we get hit with sad news soon. Pastor Cooper, the one who had advised me to leave for a while and get away from Frank, announces that he has cancer. And then a couple of weeks later, he passes away.

The tears flow down my face as Cliff and I remember his wise advice and kindness. "I can't believe he's gone."

"I think it will be hard to go back to his church, especially since we have been gone so long and he won't be there anymore" Cliff surmises. "Let's look around for another place to attend."

"Okay," I say simply.

In the next few days, we get a phone call from Madeline. It has been a month since the grueling deposition. I'm worried that we will have to go to court, so I immerse myself in the Bible and prayers. Most of the time, I feel at peace.

"Frank has decided to settle. He will pay you back every cent that you spent on therapy. He will be suspended for seven years, and when he does get to practice again, he will be under strict supervision. He won't be allowed on the board of ethics again."

Her words seep in as I try to process all she is telling me.

"Every cent?" I ask.

"Yes, we need you to go over your records and let us know how much you think it will be," she tells me.

Cliff and I go over all our receipts and calendars. We carefully compile all the records of every single session I had with Frank and how much we paid him. I feel incredibly relieved. It feels like a dream, and I cannot believe it. They heard the truth and advocated for me. They believe me. God keeps his promises to me and delivers me from my pain and suffering. It's all over, and I can finally put this behind me and move on.

Chapter 7

O ur boys have grown into young teens, and it's a joy to watch them. The first two are charismatic and ambitious, both excited for what life holds for them. The youngest is more reserved and not as eager to meet with friends or step out into an unknown world. He thrives on skateboarding, movies, and hanging around the house. All three of them have good friends, are curious about God, and are amazing sons to Cliff and me. They openly communicate what is going on in their lives and enjoy family time. We feel blessed to have them and give God the credit for all he has done in them and our family. I sometimes have days of remorse or sadness that much of the early days of their lives I spent dealing with traumatic issues. I have questions about some of that, but mostly I live a life of abundance and freedom from the dark images that plagued me for so long. I spend hours every day in the early mornings, focusing and reading God's words and practicing life-giving statements to myself. I promise God that I will follow his voice and obey him. I will nurture my relationship with him, and I will trust his lead. I am committed to a life of learning who God is and walking in freedom.

Frank had diagnosed me with dissociative identity disorder early in our therapy together. He later stated the diagnosis to only be complex post-traumatic stress disorder and attributed the dissociation to this diagnosis. I struggle with his assessments and finally decide that I will not attach my identity to any of his conclusions. God did not design me with these labels or diagnosis, so in response to God I decide that who I am is only determined by what God says about me. I learn more about flashbacks, memories, and childhood trauma. I feel more settled on the memories that are true, but there are others that confound me. For instance, I still cannot remember a significant portion of my childhood. When I think back on certain ages, it is a total blank even to this day. I conclude that it is not for me to know right now, God holds the past and the future, I just need to live in the present. With this decision, remaining confusion leaves and I am at a place of surrender. I cultivate the belief that God will turn my negative life experiences into something positive.

As I surrender daily to God, and I believe what He has to say about me, my perspective on life changes. The internal dialogue I have with myself also changes. If the images present themselves, I learn to stop them by feeding myself with the wonderful words God says. Peace and calm continue to overtake my daily life, and I am hopeful about all that is to come.

Now that the boys are older and doing so much on their own Cliff asks me what I want to do in the years ahead. I've spent years as a stay-at-home mom pouring my energy into each of their lives and devoting my life to their happiness.

"I'd like to have another baby." I answer him with a sly smile. "I love our boys. So much of my time raising them was marked with my own trauma, now I want to have a child and raise him in peace."

"Really?" Cliff responds, he is surprised. We are both in our late thirties and understand that getting pregnant may not come as easily as the first three did. To add to the complication of age we must deal with the vasectomy that Cliff had several years ago. We both know that this may make my desire impossible. "This is a lot to think about! I'm not sure I want to do little babies all over again." Cliff honestly responds. "We just got the boys at a place where they are doing their own laundry and are self-sufficient.

Now, they just need to finish high school and college, and we will be kid-free!" he says.

"I know. It is a lot for you, as it requires you to have a vasectomy reversal. I know it's not a small matter and it is a huge commitment, but we are only in our thirties, we will still be young when this child is grown." I smile.

Cliff agrees to see a doctor and at least find out what the chances are with a reversal. If the chance is good, then he is willing to move ahead with another child.

We also meet with my doctor, who helped birth our boys years ago. I tell her what we have decided, and she is excited to help us bring another child into the world.

The doctor tells Cliff that it is possible, but not a guarantee. He tells us that we may be able to get pregnant six months after the reversal, but it is likely to take much longer. "Alright." Cliff says in a somewhat resigned tone. "I'll go ahead with the surgery."

I am elated. Of course, after three boys I hope for a girl, but also surrender that to God and promise to be thrilled either way. "God, it is your domain, and you know what is best for our family" I pray in earnest.

Six months later I take a pregnancy test and much to my delight, I am pregnant. "Guess what? We did it! We are going to have another baby!" I announce to Cliff excitedly.

The happiness and joy we feel is unexplainable. The boys join us in the upcoming anticipation. Our youngest sews a blanket for the baby. We have fun as a family discussing names and decide that each boy will pick a name for their brother or sister. It must be parent approved of course!

Our fourth son is born on a snowy winter day through a C-section. After our teary welcome as parents, all three brothers envelop the new baby and shower him with love. They take the job of being elder brothers very seriously. It turns out to be one of the best days of my life. We have a big party at the hospital with a happy birthday sign pinned to the wall and a cake. The boy's shop for a little outfit their brother can wear home from the hospital, and we wrap him snuggly in his brother made blanket. I feel so proud of my sons and the immediate investment they make in their new brother.

"This feels amazing!" I tell Cliff as he drives us from the hospital. "We have the best baby ever. I want to do this again so he will have a sibling," I laugh as I catch Cliff's eye.

"I'll have to think about that," he smiles back at me.

My life feels full and busy at the same time. I love having a new baby. My heart-mom, Lucy, visits for the birth and stays a couple weeks after we arrive home. She loves washing all the little clothes we have and spending time with our new addition. The brothers are mesmerized by him. We all feel joyful and excited. I see that he is a gift from God, and I am grateful. I continue to focus on Godly thoughts and devote more of my emotions and self to God –surrender becomes my daily goal as I lean into relationship with God above all else.

"I met the sister of a childhood friend today," I casually tell Cliff as I clean up after changing the baby's diaper. "She has two little girls. We are going to start walking together in the mornings with the kids." I feel excited.

"That will be great for you. What's her name?" Cliff responds.

"Her name is Ellie. She's the little sister of my friend, Seth. In fact, I remember the day she was born," I reminisce. "Anyway, she's coming over tomorrow morning, and we are taking the kids out for a neighborhood walk."

Ellie and I instantly enjoy each other's company. We have the connection of being raised in the same church and knowing many of the same people. My mother worked for Ellie's family for years. We walk around the neighborhood a couple of times a week. I feel delighted to have her in my life, as well as her girls. We sometimes do other fun things together as well. We both enjoy the moment and our budding friendship. Just like that, two years have passed, and our new baby is already two-years-old. Cliff and I decide to have another child because I want our baby to have someone close to his age. And lo and behold, I get pregnant right away.

"I'm pregnant again," I say with a smile one morning as Ellie and I take a walk.

"Oh, that's wonderful!" she exclaims, her face beaming.

Deep down inside, I know that it's another boy. I love having sons, and I feel excited for the boys to have another sibling to grow up with. But then, at 24 weeks pregnant, I have a horrifying dream. I dream that our baby is dead in the womb. I wake up trembling with terror and immediately wake Cliff up. I just know something is wrong.

"Cliff, we need to go to the doctor!" I cry out. "I had a

dream that the baby died. I feel like something is very different, and I need to hear the heartbeat."

I call the clinic and tell them that I believe something is wrong. They ask us to come in at 10 AM when our doctor is available. I anxiously wait in the waiting room before seeing the doctor.

"Oh God! I am afraid of how this is going to turn out. I love this child, but I feel as if I will not raise him. With great pain, I surrender him to you! At the same time, please let me hear his heartbeat. Please!"

"I just know something is wrong," I say fearfully as we wait for the doctor to call us in.

"It's going to be okay," Cliff assures me and holds my hand tightly.

Then we are ushered into the exam room, the doctor patiently moves the doppler across my belly to hear the heartbeat. It feels like she does this for a very long time, and the look on her face is somber.

"I'm not hearing it right now. It could just be the position he is in, but at 24 weeks, we should be able to hear," she says cautiously. "Let's look at the ultrasound."

I feel a doom rest upon me and realize that if he is alive, it will be a miracle. I feel deep distress.

Cliff and I hold our breath as the technician rubs the cold gel over my belly. The room grows silent as she slides the transducer all around, trying to catch the heartbeat. She looks at the doctor after a while and shakes her head. Our baby boy has no heartbeat. I burst into tears and look at the screen. The image on the screen is the same one that I saw in my dream. The pain is piercing my heart, and I can't breathe. It feels like my heart will stop. Heaviness crashes over me as I lay crying on the bed.

"We need to admit you to the hospital soon to deliver your baby." the doctor explains. "We will induce labor, and you can deliver him normally, and then say goodbye to him." She strokes my hair and tries to calm me.

"God was preparing me," I say as Cliff drives me home. "It doesn't necessarily ease the pain, but for some reason, he was telling me. And now, we have a dead baby to deliver. I don't think I can do this, Cliff!"

"Yes, you can. You are so strong and brave. I won't ever leave your side," Cliff promises me.

I am admitted to the hospital the next morning. The nurses are gentle enough to stay silent while they pump my veins with meds. I am in a beautiful suite at the hospital. It's big with enough room for Cliff to rest as well. We have complete privacy and quiet.

"This is a small dose to start, then we will gradually increase it until you have delivered." The kind nurse explains to me.

We wait without saying a word to each other. We are both lost in our thoughts about how to move on from such a tragedy. And then the labor begins. The contractions come rapidly, one after another. The physical pain combined with the emotional pain is exhausting. "I don't want to do this!" I cry.

"It's okay, just a couple of pushes, and you will be done," the doctor encourages.

After a few hours, I give birth to a tiny handful of a baby boy. He is perfect. I stare at him in shock and wish I could bring life back to him.

"Do you want to hold him?" the doctor asks as she holds the tiny bundle of human in her hand.

"Yes," I mumble and reach out my hand for him. I stare at him and whisper, "He looks so perfect! If only he were breathing. If only."

I hold him in the palm of my hand and weep for the loss for what seems like days. I hold him and tell him that I love him, and I will miss him so much. The nurse brings in a lovely box inlaid with a blanket and asks us if we want to lay him there for the burial.

"Okay," I utter weakly and lay him down in the box. "I will see you again someday, little man." I gently whisper. "Remember your name, Abel John." I carefully lay him in the tiny box.

The weeks that follow only drift in and out of my consciousness. I drive to a coffee shop with our toddler and just sit there with him. I feel sad and confused. Sometimes I ask myself, "How could this have happened? Why would he just die?" I feel alone and awkward around people because I don't know what to say. I can't stand the superficial, caring ways and the pity that resides in their eyes. The pain I feel is uncomfortable for those around me, and I retreat to the safety of my own home and family.

"I'm not ready to go to church," I say to Cliff as I curl into a ball on the bed. "It hurts too much to be with people right now."

My doctor tells us that there is no reason we can't conceive again. "You can try again and have a normal, happy baby," she tells us. "Just wait 4 to 6 months and then try again."

Her assurance gives us hope, and we do just that. After a few months, Cliff and I try again for a baby. I get pregnant in the next five months. But we end up losing that baby as well. We get pregnant three more times over the next couple of years, and every single time, I lose them. There is no explanation for the losses. I am healthy, the lost babies were healthy. It appears that it is not meant to be.

"I can't do this anymore!" I sigh with exhaustion. "I don't understand why our babies are dying, especially when we are told that there is nothing wrong with them or with me!"

"You talked before about adopting. Let's do that," Cliff comforts me.

"Are you sure?" I ask him.

"Yes!" Cliff says.

Immediately, after we decide to adopt, we contact an adoption agency. We choose to adopt a baby girl from China, because the three older boys say they want a sister. The agency informs us that it will take 9 to 12 months. When our youngest is four years old, we travel to China to bring home our 18-month-old daughter. We are excited and so thankful for all the ways God redeems our losses.

"See you in two weeks! I can't wait to meet her!" The boys call out to us at the airport, and we head inside towards the terminal.

We arrive in Shanghai, and our guide is waiting for us at the airport. He has a sign with our name on it, and a big smile on his face. He speaks impeccable English, and we immediately connect with him and like him. He drives us to the hotel and says, "Get a good night's sleep. Tomorrow we will drive North to the next city where you will meet your new daughter!"

The entire trip is a whirlwind as we sign document after document, travel from one city to the next. On our third day in China, we chart a bus to go to the government office with other expecting parents to meet our baby girl. The anticipation is overwhelming. We don't know exactly what to expect, we just follow our guide and listen carefully to his instructions. We stop by an open door and our guide tells us that our babies are inside. Each expectant parent wants to look through the door into the room. We finally get our turn and inside the room are several adults, all holding little girls or babies on their laps. One little girl toddles around the room with her nanny in close pursuit. She has a big smile on her face.

"There she is!" Cliff points to a little girl who is sitting quietly on the nanny's lap.

"I don't think that's her," I say and point to the bubbly little girl toddling around the room. Our guide invites us into the room, and we discover that the very girl I had spotted earlier turns out to be our daughter. She now sits on her nanny's lap playing peek-a-boo with our four-year-old son. The picture of them together melts my heart and I am overjoyed.

"You can now take your babies," the guide tells the parents.

The nanny hands over my daughter to me. I comfort her by saying, "Oh, it's going to be okay. I know this is very scary and new for you."

After screaming and protesting loudly, she begins to quiet and looks around. Then she clings to me and looks warily at Cliff and our son. She is not initially happy to be with either of them, she hasn't seen many males before, and it feels scary to her. It was safe to enjoy our four- year- old at a distance but as she realizes that her life is changing and he will be with her all the time, her fear increases.

We too are unsure of what to do. I was unprepared for such a dramatic response, but as I think about it, I begin to understand. This small child has only known her nanny for 18 months, and now strangers come in and simply take her away from who she knows and loves. It is scary.

"I feel like we are living in a dream right now." I comment. "We have a daughter, she is ours!"

Our daughter is a beautiful addition to our family. She is our little bookend. I feel content and happy. With each day, life gets better. My children, husband, and I have more good days than bad. The losses I have faced sometimes surface, but I let go of the anger and frustration and lean into my growing faith in Jesus. The loss of Jocelyn, Eleanor,

Mildred, Ingrid, Janet, and Liz is a distant memory, something I strive to learn from. I question what I could've done differently. At the time I did attempt to reach out to them all, but the relationships had been ruined by awkwardness, judgment, and mistrust.

My time with God is sweet, and when I pray, I feel a deep connection. The hours I lean into Him become more and more precious and life-giving.

"I believe that prayer is my greatest weapon and guarantee for experiencing a successful day." I share with Cliff one day. "I've been spending a lot of time noting down my prayers and quietly sitting before God waiting for His response. It's also helpful to give all my thoughts to Him intentionally. I feel so good!"

When I face images from my past, I pray for relief and truth from Jesus. And the more I focus on his truth and him being my reality, I can let go of the darkness. It isn't always easy, of course. But I am growing in my knowledge and self-discipline. I pour over Beth Moore studies and find freedom in her Breaking Free from childhood abuse study. I gain clarity on my responses to different events and situations in life and confirm that they are flashbacks from my childhood.

And daily, I give back to Jesus.

I feel like I am making progress, slow progress. I believe that God is interested in my journey, and He wants to heal my mind. The images, the fear, the pain; it all means something. I'm surrendering it more to Jesus, even when I don't totally understand it. People heal. I will continue to heal. I will be strong and courageous and will not allow my past to determine my present.

My journal is still a constant companion. I sort out my thoughts and feelings and write down my prayers. Every morning, I wake up early and read my Bible; I listen to the voice of God. It is clearer to me who God says He is and who He says I am. It feels good.

"Let's visit that new church this Sunday," Cliff suggests to me one evening.

"Okay. I'm ready to try it out," I agree.

When Sunday arrives, we pile the kids in our car and head to the next town. It was the only huge church in the vicinity. We are excited and eager to check it out. We once heard the pastor preach on the radio, and his topics were engaging, and we believe he is a true man of God.

"Wow! This is big," I say, staring wide-eyed at the church after we park the car.

We settle the kids in their appropriate classes and go to the sanctuary.

"Welcome!" says a kind woman who greets us at the double doors that lead to the large room. We smile, take the pamphlets she offers, and take our seats. There are many people around us, but deep down, I feel that we have found our home.

"So, what did you think?" I turn to Cliff as we drive away to find somewhere to have lunch.

"It was good. So different from the church we grew up in. It feels good in there!" Cliff says.

We continue discussing the differences we found, contrasting the new church and the extremely legalistic one we grew up in. We both left the conservative legalistic church from our childhood, but we have not yet been able to find a church to call home since Pastor Cooper passed away years earlier. We visit some places but don't settle. But this one feels like an excellent place to settle.

Both Cliff and I grow in relationship with God. We pray

regularly, we believe it is a lifeline and the best way to connect with God. I learn that the negativity in my head was not my own but from the enemy, which is a battle that I can only win through prayer.

"Prayer really is a secret weapon," I muse as we come back from church. "It brings me more peace and clarity. When I pray it gives me clarity on how to approach life. It's amazing to me!"

I feel giddy at the prospect. We continue to attend the big church every week. We meet new people who are friendly and helpful. Our children thrive, and so do we. One morning, we make our way into the church and sit down, I notice something startling. "Frank is sitting two people down from us!" I whisper in Cliff's ear.

Frank sits with his wife, both staring straight ahead as if doing their best to avoid eye contact with me. We make it through the rest of the service. As the people are dismissed, Frank and his wife go out one way while Cliff and I take another way. As I enter the foyer, I see Frank directly in front of me. At this point he is unavoidable, and I feel anger seep up inside me. I walk closer to him and boldly comment, "I've made a lot of mistakes in my life," I say. "Seeing you as a counselor was one of them. Still, I want to apologize, mostly to your wife for any part that I had in a destructive relationship with you."

I briefly look at his wife, Audrey, and then back to Frank, "I think a lot of the pain that came from seeing you could've been avoided if you had just admitted the truth and apologized." I stare at Frank for a moment and then walk away. He and his wife dart out a side door.

Years go by, we are now established in the church. We go to a connect group every week to be with other families. The group grows so much so that it splits into two groups. Cliff and I are asked to become leaders of a connect group. We accept and then move to a new group to be leaders every week.

But around the same time, it is evident that I am not an actual leader because women are not allowed to lead men. I am only there to support Cliff as he leads. I feel confused about that and believe in my heart that God has much more intended for women.

"I know there are texts in the Bible that say women need to be silent, there are also texts that say we are all equal. And there are a lot of women leaders in the Bible," I say out loud as Cliff, and I drive home one day. "It feels like I must choose between leadership and being in a church we love. Ultimately, it's how God sees it and what he wants."

I decide that I will devote some prayer and study to this topic and see what I can discover.

I find some books on women in leadership, and I'm introduced to an entirely new world. I search for the author of one book and find that he is a pastor of a church in California. I begin to listen to his sermons and to the music they produce. I am thrilled by the belief system and how it lines up with the spoken Word of God.

"Maybe you can find a place in women's ministry," Cliff suggests.

"Maybe, but that doesn't change the core belief that I'm not equal to you in God's eyes," I say with finality.

Cliff's suggestion sticks with me, and I decide to join a women's group supporting women who have faced sexual abuse. I find that I have a deep understanding of what many of the women are revealing and experiencing. I remember feeling much the same way when dealing with images and troubling thoughts. The group leader acknowledges my work and asks me to co-lead another group with her. She considers me a good leader with compassion and understanding for the ladies. Of course, I readily accept.

I do feel great compassion and connection for women who have faced abuse. The women I meet in the church tell me stories of how they were preyed upon. Some were abused by their partners, a friend or family member whom they trusted the most. Some tell stories of how they were abused in the ministry. It compels me to become a source of comfort and peace for them. I pray to God about how He wants me to contribute to their recovery and healing. I continue to pray to God so that if He wants me to know more about my past, He will help me remember.

Chapter 8

I t is said that time heals all wounds. With time you gain maturity, patience, and a better perspective on life. I have spent years recovering from childhood trauma, but it isn't just time that brings healing. It is discipline, grit, and a yearning for the power of God to bring healing. It is with God that the healing begins. It is with the acceptance of who he is, and who he creates us to be. It is with our destined identity woven deep within our very being that the healing begins. After years, I finally find myself in a place where I am at peace and free from the images that once tormented my mind. It has been years since I left Frank and therapy. Years since I last saw or spoke to my friends that I went to Europe with. My life is calm and tranquil.

I am secure in my relationship with God. I diligently look for more of him and stay connected in prayer. I trust the healing power of God and all His promises. He will do what he says he will do. I feel his presence with me. I long for more of him.

However, even in a time of peace, pain can come. It is the

way that pain is processed that makes a difference for me. When there is trauma, there are scars. Scars are a reminder of all that happened, but also a reminder of the redemptive power of Jesus.

There are times I think of my time with Frank, and the feelings that followed. I have not confided in others the depth of my experiences with him. God and Cliff remain the true holders of my heart and all that entails. I struggle with words often and find it a challenge to talk. I feel blocked in many ways from the words that describe the intensity of my experience. There are times I think I am the only one, and if I confide in someone I will be rejected.

I am not sure I understand all of it, so how can anyone else? Shame occasionally creeps in when I think of Frank, and I intentionally learn to take it to God. How can anyone begin to comprehend the extent of this? Is there anyone that can understand my belief that my healing is all because of the focus on God and his truth?

With the stacking of one year upon another, I strengthen my focus and attention on God. I focus on identity in him and see that every problem in life stems from a lack of identity in Jesus. If we do not understand who we are and believe it, issues occur. Resolution forms in my mind when I wrestle with disturbing thoughts or memories. I pray for revelation of where Jesus was during those formative years. What was he thinking? How does he plan to turn all the pain into good?

I remember the struggle I had with reality and the constant questions of being real myself. I thank God for changing that in my life and giving me understanding that he is reality. I mull the word 'real' over in my mind and ask myself what it means to me. I pray for God to explain it to me. I conclude that 'real' is an acronym. When I am rooted in Jesus Christ and listen to his Spirit, I am then empowered to live a bold and authentic life, which in turn enables me to love and be loved. Rooted. Empowered. Authentic. Loved. That is real.

I feel purpose when I listen to and mentor other women who suffer like me or went through similar struggles in life. I know that God gives me the ability to listen and then understand them, mostly because I can relate to their hardships and feelings. Peace continues to ensue to the point that others point out how peaceful I am. God shines through in ways I don't see, but others do.

I see that God is turning my pain into good by using me to be there for others. He is using my voice to bring hope, connection, and love. If I hadn't experienced such intense lack and abuse; understanding others would be impossible. I find myself being thankful for the lessons I learn in life from all the experience.

Stories from other women pile in and I see that I am not alone. I feel more confident in reaching out to others in similar roles and seeking friendship. I want to learn more about leadership and be the best I can in helping others.

Hazel, the new women's ministry leader for my church, is from the Midwest. She is there to build a stronger women's ministry within the church.

Hazel is a lean dark-haired woman with an athletic build and bright green eyes. The first time I meet Hazel is at our Bible group, she joins us, and I, along with the others, are happy to have her. She's friendly enough, but also has a clear emotional wall that keeps the group at arm's length.

I do like her, though, and understand how hard it can be to get to know new people. I decide to step out of my comfort zone and reach out to her while we are at church. I want to get to know her and be friends with her.

It's helpful that she is in our Bible group. We have dinners together, play games, enjoy each other as a group. Gradually, we occasionally meet at church before the service. We sit in the foyer and talk, each time we learn a little more about each other.

After a few months, Hazel and I go for walks, meet for coffee, and hang out at the park. We get to know each other as I ask her about her life, family, and living in the Midwest. She tells me she was once married, but tragically lost her husband in an accident. She raised a child on her own, until one day he died as well. It is clear to me that she is in pain, and it is difficult to share these topics. I feel honored that she trusts me with her story. She asks me about my life and my family.

We have fun together, but I still feel the wall between us. I surmise that she too has experienced untold pain, and it is challenging to trust at a deep level. Still, I work to trust her, and I do feel comfortable with her. I share some of the struggles in my life, and touch on the story of memories and pain that were mine for many years. I admit to living in confusion for years and the long journey God has led me on to recover.

I share some of the memories I had so determinedly worked through with Frank and talk about my struggles with my mother now and the memory of my mother and people from the church praying over me.

As the relationship deepens, I tell her about the court settlement and how I felt back then. I do not share my therapy experiences but make it clear I do not intend to do go to therapy again. I share my experience of surrender to God and how He brings me relief, and comfort after years of questioning Him, and I share my doubts about his love for me being real.

I cautiously ask her questions about herself, as she keeps her answers vague. I approach her slowly so as not to push her away. I notice that there are times I feel inferior when I am around her and ponder what the root of that is. Is it my own experiences in life or things she says to me? I shrug the doubts away choosing to pursue trust in friendship.

Hazel and I continue to meet once a week and enjoy the company of each other. We both feel more comfortable in our friendship, so when a conference comes up in a nearby city, I invite her along. She agrees, and I book the hotel room, get the tickets, and discuss places where we can eat.

We arrive before the evening session and check into the hotel, then go out to eat dinner. We start to unpack after we come back to our hotel, chatting lightly. That is when I come upon something in my bag; I didn't pack it. In fact, I haven't seen it in years. It is tucked away in the pocket of the suitcase I pull it out and see a drawing that I made years ago while I was still seeing Frank.

At the time, when in therapy with Frank, I had drawn it to visualize his version of my brain being several different rooms. My hope was that the drawing would help me have a better understanding of the chaos inside of me. I mention the drawing to Hazel as she unpacks her stuff. She asks to see it, and we sit down on the bedside as I show it to her.

Lines and numbers meet up with words of chaos and agony. It's like a big chart with questions, memories, and scribbles that were once embedded in my heart. Hazel mentions the incident involving my mom and the church elders that prayed over me.

I begin to feel a heavy tension in the room. She rests her

hand on my back and starts to pray. As soon as she starts to pray, I am cautious about her motives. I focus on the prayer, but the walls are closing in on me. I feel a little dizzy and foggy.

Her prayer is just like the church elders many years ago. She forcefully demands the demons leave my body. I feel like I have been transported back in time, and I am back to the scared little girl. My head spins, and I feel sick.

"Get away from me," I demand as my head spins.

She ignores me completely and continues to pray without stopping. She reaches out both of her hands and places them on me, pressing hard as if trying to force her perceived "demons" away from me.

I feel scared and angry. I push her away from me, demanding that she leave me alone. I am too angry to say anything, I go to the other bed, curl up, and lay in silence. She walks into the bathroom, cloaked in shame and fear.

Later, I call Cliff as I am too restless to go to sleep. I tell him what happened and how Hazel prayed over me. He gets furious at Hazel and asks me how I am. I regret sharing the drawing and wish the weekend were over.

The next day, we both go to the conference. We are both exhausted and only manage to chit-chat feebly without mentioning last night's episode. I feel the tension between us but choose to ignore it. We don't discuss her praying over me or how I reacted to it. I want to, but I cannot trust her anymore. I feel unsure of what she will do next. The day stretches on, and I notice a couple women staring at me and whispering. I later find out that the two women are good friends with Hazel, and she called them at some point before the morning session and told them all that had occurred. The end of the conference has not come soon enough. It is a relief to me to drive home, leaving Hazel at her own house.

The days after the conference are tense and fitful. Since that night, we have not spoken to each other, and I don't want to. I struggle to find my equilibrium and spend hours asking God about what occurred. I am sad that my own response was so intense and disappointed that I did not handle it better.

A few weeks passed and I receive an email from Hazel. She tells me that she cannot meet with me anymore. She says she has work to do, and she also does not feel safe being with me. She tells me that I manipulate her and that I am mean.

Her list goes on, and I feel a little stunned by all her accusations. I bring it all to Jesus and ask him to reveal to me mistakes I may not see and show me a better way. I repent of my own wrongdoing. I beg God for some kind of resolution in my heart with Hazel, I also plead with God to let me leave the friendship in peace. I am not interested in entering back into a relationship with Hazel. I earnestly pray for wise women to be in my life, for faithful loyal friendships. I ask God to teach me appropriate boundaries in my relationships.

One night, I have a dream. I am sitting on a stool outside the church. When I look at the upper window, I spot Hazel looking out the window directly at me. Then I turn my gaze to look beside the church and see a line of beautifully dressed women coming out from the back of the church. They do not approach me but go towards the large dumpster.

The women start to pull garbage out of the dumpster and smear it all over themselves. I call for them to stop, to wait. I tell them I want to help them; they don't have to put garbage on themselves! But then I see Hazel close the curtain of the window and walk away. I run to the sides of the church and to the back to find a way in, but I see no doors. I finally

WHEN THE CHURCH THINKS YOU'RE CRAZY

find a door that looks like it leads to a cellar of sorts. I try to pry it open, but it won't budge. I wake up with a deep conviction that this dream is from God.

I think a lot about the dream and tell Maddy, my prayer partner, and friend. Maddy and I have been praying together for months now. She too is going through her own trials, and we have been there for each other.

I ponder the dream and wonder if God is telling me that I will help women outside of the church; I need to prepare to be left out. I have little idea how painful the experience will be and how it will test my strength and faith in the church.

I recall a time that I am at another women's conference years earlier. I enter the large stadium and sit down to hear a prominent woman speaker. As I look over the thousands of women in attendance, I distinctly hear in my mind that I, too, will someday speak for God. I do not understand exactly what that will look like.

The thought of that is intimidating at the time. I try to push it away, but it only becomes stronger. From that day, the knowledge of speaking for God increases in my mind, and I believe it is a thought directly from him. It is certainly not my own thinking!

Meanwhile, after we return from the conference, Hazel proceeds to confide in the church elders about that night. She tells them that I am not safe and that I terrify her. She says that I am a danger to women and children in the church.

She tells them about how she prayed over me. She believes she had to, and it was a spiritual battle that scared her more than any experience before. From what I can tell, she leads them to believe that instead of the story I share with her being in my past, she declares it a present danger. She informs them that fear, chaos, and dark images are all a part of my current daily life. They advise her to step away from the relationship because I am, in their opinion, crazy.

She calls Cliff and asks to meet with him. He agrees to meet with her but doesn't want to meet her one on one. He doesn't trust her. He is relieved to see that our friend Don, from the church, joins them in the meeting.

During their meeting, Hazel tells him that I am sick and that I need counseling. He defends me by saying that I have already worked through the issues that she claims are still present. And her behavior is inexcusable towards anyone that has dealt with PTSD.

She proceeds to tell my husband that I will not be a fruitful Christian and will fail at anything I try to do. She insists that people, in general, should be wary of me because she thinks I will hurt them, especially children and women, due to my "issues." Cliff is frustrated with her; he tells Hazel that she isn't a good friend.

They think I am crazy and claim
that I cannot possibly have a relationship
with God.

Not surprisingly, the church leaders organize meetings regarding me and Hazel's claims about me. They think I am crazy and claim that I cannot possibly have a relationship with God. Don remains supportive as Cliff, and I try to navigate the toxicity and negativity of the treatment of many of the church leaders and Hazel's absence.

Pastors fight over how Cliff, and I are being treated. Hazel insists that I seek professional advice for my mental health. Preston, a church leader, jumps to my defense and pleads with his co-workers to listen.

He is shocked to hear and see how church leaders treat Cliff and me after having spent so many years together growing and progressing with them in our relationship with God. I feel frustrated and sad. Both Cliff and I feel shunned by the church leadership. We devote a lot of time in prayer. We want to understand what to do next.

I think of my recent dream and ask God to give me the ability to trust that he will use me and my life experiences outside of the church walls. I ask him to give me compassion towards Hazel, even though the current pain gives me cause to never be in a friendship with her again.

I vacillate between anger and sadness as I watch the years in this church family be uprooted by the leaders' unkind and judgmental words and actions. I cry out to God for freedom from the consequences of my past.

Cliff and I decide to try to do all that is being asked of us through the church leadership; we want to honor God's church. We make an appointment with a prominent Christian leader to get an assessment.

I am hopeful that if a well-known Christian leader knows

about PTSD and disassociation and gives his opinion, then the leaders in my church will have a clearer understanding of why I responded the way that I did that evening. I also apply helpful steps to take so that I can respond calmly when triggered with a painful memory again.

Numerous friends send letters to the lead pastor. They testify of my stability and recall how I have helped them find Jesus and friendship over the years. I am touched by the letters and believe it will help.

I want to gain their trust again and move on with our lives. Preston tells us that Hazel is not stable or liked. He claims that she is difficult to work with, and the staff walks on eggshells when with her.

I am saddened by the events that are out of my control, and I am surprised that no number of letters or professional opinion changes the mindset of what they have already determined about me.

Chapter 9

My life with Cliff is strong and steady. My sweet, devoted husband never leaves my side. His undying love and support anchors me during the toughest of times. When I think about him and how far he has come with me, I believe his love is his best quality.

Cliff originally lived in Canada, growing up with his immigrant parents, who came from Holland. With two older siblings, Cliff is the baby of his family. His parents speak both English and Dutch, which can cause confusion sometimes when it comes to communication.

Cliff blurts things out that are either too much or unfavorable. Despite that, he always loves me deeply and shows me his love thoughtfully and tenderly. Through all the ups and downs, therapy, PTSD, and abandoning friends, Cliff remains steadfast, loyal, and kind to me.

Early in our marriage he deals with life in a passive way, not allowing turmoil to steer him off course. He does not like confrontation. There are times I need this as my emotions are all over the place. He remains unwavering. As much as it saves him from getting into unwanted situations, it does not always work when it comes to our marriage. I prefer a more relatable stance with clear direction.

So, when the issues arise at church, Cliff is forced to take a stance. The words and actions of the church leaders cause him to step his game up a bit. The situation isn't favorable, and he knows we cannot solve it by remaining passive. He knows that this is one of those moments where he must speak up because it concerns me and the truth.

His love for me trumps his fear of confrontation. So, he takes on the role of a defender. Through it all, the hurtful actions and words of everyone, I grow and learn more about the world. I experience the harshness and cruelty that is present in all of us, fortunately, not everyone utilizes it.

But it isn't just me who grows and learns a few things. Cliff also does some growing of his own. He comes out shining on the other end, proving himself to be an amazing man, husband, and father.

As for Hazel, I am betrayed and hurt beyond imagination. But more than anything, the anger I feel is directed at myself.

I feel foolish for believing that I could tell someone my story and experiences and expect them to remain in my life. How can they, after finding out all the twisted details of my life? All I can find myself doing is praying to God for His guidance over the next steps. I ask Him to enable me to trust that He brings people in my life that do not judge me by my past.

While praying, I feel like God is asking me to reconcile with Hazel. I feel deep inside that God is asking me to pursue a renewed friendship. Every time I pray to God, asking for His help and guidance, a particular verse from the Bible pops in my head:

> *"If you've gotten anything at all out of following Christ, if his love has made any difference in your life, if being in a community of the Spirit means anything to you, if you have a heart, if you care-then do me a favor: Agree with each other, love each other, be deep-spirited friends." - **Philippians 2:1-2 (MSG)***

So, in obedience, I go to church every week to rebuild my friendship with Hazel. We meet regularly, and even though she seems hesitant, we both come around to talk about the betrayal we felt. We discuss our points of view. It becomes clear to me soon enough that we will never see eye-to-eye on the subject. In Hazel's opinion, my past was not reconciled and is my present.

However, God heals my thought process daily and continues to do a good work in me. He healed me to the degree that I can help others in their pain and struggles. The process of forgiving Hazel is hard and takes surrender to the will of God. But I pray daily for God to use me in her life in such a way that our friendship can heal along with our hearts.

We gradually rebuild and restore over the next year. We meet outside of the church, and we meet up regularly. We go for walks, get coffee together, or have a nice dinner where we talk about life experiences. We both work on our own set of church issues and the relationship dynamics that changed due to the whole debacle.

Hazel tells me how her life has changed drastically, as well. She confides in me that she isn't safe in her work environment anymore. She tells me she feels confined. She does not feel safe with the new women's ministry leader. It prompts me to think about a dream. The dream clarifies to me that God is working with all of us to grow and change.

In my dream, I see Hazel inside a tomb. She is lying on a slab of stone wrapped up like a mummy. Her eyes are closed as if she were in a deep sleep. She can't move or do anything. Then I see Jesus himself standing by her feet. He smiles at me, which gives me peace and comfort. Then he starts unwrapping the cloth from around Hazel's body.

I realize that Hazel responds to me out of her own pain and fear. She may be a pastor, but she is not healthy. She too has issues to work through and being with me in that hotel room triggered her as well. She lost her position at work because of her actions; that cannot be easy. We both face changes in our lives. She is not the women's ministry pastor in the church but given a different position where she spends most of her time alone working on projects.

Both Cliff and I are told that a call was put to the senior Pastor advising that Hazel be moved to a less interactive position. Shortly after this occurs, Pastor Preston approaches me. He was one of the few loyal supporters Cliff and I had when the church leaders turned against us.

Pastor Preston asks me to organize and speak at a women's dinner. He says he advocates for me and wants me to coordinate the church event in a different district. I feel honored at his words and faith in my abilities. I happily accept his generous offer and set out to plan the event meticulously. I put together a team to cook, decorate, and prepare for the dinner. I am in my element, and I'm grateful God is giving me this opportunity.

Three short weeks later, with over 150 ladies in attendance, the women's dinner is well underway. Everyone enjoys the food, company, and the presentation I give. They applaud me after my talk, and I feel a sense of accomplishment and joy settle in my heart. It is a highlight of my year. I feel excited, and the entire night goes perfectly.

I talk to the ladies about the many travels we have in life and the unexpected events it brings. I call my speech "Traveling Shoes" I use several pairs of shoes as a display and share the impact that events and people have on our life. At the end of my talk, I pull out a scarf and wrap it around one of the lady's necks. "This is our traveling scarf." I say with a smile. "When you have enjoyed this scarf for a couple of weeks then please pass it on to another lady and remind her to do the same." All the women love the idea and have fun for weeks sharing the Traveling Scarf. We add to the fun at the next dinner by presenting a Bible to be passed from one woman to the next after they find their favorite verse and comment on it in the Bible.

After the massive success of the dinner we organize, the Pastor gives me responsibility for another one. Everyone wants to see the dinners continue and so we plan another one next month. More women attend, and ministry leaders from other churches come as well. The new women's ministry leader, Karen, tells me she wants to meet with me. We set up a time to meet for lunch.

Since Hazel was women's ministry leader, Karen has a lot to say about her. She comments on her inability to run a ministry. Hazel is my friend, it's not the same as before, but I believe God will bless our friendship because I have pursued her as a deep-spirited friend.

Later, the responsibility of the women's ministry dinner is handed to someone else. Karen does not want me to be involved and asks someone else to take over. I am disappointed. I choose to believe that God has His hand in everything, and I am at peace with this decision. I believe this has something to do with everything that has happened over the past year with the church leaders and Hazel.

I still attend the next dinner and notice that the attendance is down by half. It is a disappointing failure, and the event is canceled altogether. It is a short-lived monthly event. I am grateful for the times I was involved.

I know I am called to speak into the hearts of women. I am called to support them when they experience difficult times. It has become very clear to me that I will not be doing that within the church walls.

I begin to focus on the proper training I need so that I have the skills to lead women to a place of freedom. The church's leadership is not supportive of me doing any kind of ministry outside of their supervision. Yet, they will not allow me to do anything within the church either. So, I continue in the way I believe God is calling me. I spend more time with Maddy, my friend and prayer partner. We soon travel together for training and begin the process of helping others. We lean on each other for support during the difficult time at church.

Meanwhile, the women's ministry leader does not give up

on talking bad about Hazel. She keeps trash-talking her, and then her attention is shifted towards me. She starts lashing out at me and accuses me of lying about how she asked me to organize the dinners. She tells me she knows all about my past and cannot rely on a word that I say. I say nothing and refuse to fuel the fire any further.

On the other hand, my friendship with Hazel grows. We become close enough that she confides about the work environment she faces. She tells me how she felt all that time ago when she went to the church leaders concerning our evening at the hotel. She relays how it made her feel after she told them my story. Our friendship begins to thrive, with both of us leaving any ill feelings about each other in the past.

As the years pass, I ponder over my friendship with Hazel. God has done a miraculous healing between the two of us. We meet weekly, grab some food or coffee, and hang out as regular friends do. We do a lot together, but it is nowhere near what I imagined our friendship to be, especially after so many years.

There is still a distance, a wall, between us that keeps her from getting close to my family or other friends. One day, when I broach the subject with her quite hesitantly, she admits to me that she hasn't told anyone at the church about our friendship all these years. She doesn't want anyone to know that we hang out.

And so, after all the prayers, tears, anger, pain, and sorrow, Cliff and I decide to leave the congregation for good. When we joined, it was a place for us to feel safe, to feel at home. A place where we thought we belonged. But now, after all our friends have left as well, it does not feel like that anymore. We do not feel safe with the leadership, and we don't belong with them. It's not a place where we can grow as faithful followers of God. We put in a lot of effort and time to work things out with the leaders. We tried to fix what had been broken, not through any fault of our own. We tried to do what leadership asked, only to discover that they did not have any faith in our abilities. The atmosphere was oppressive, and it was time for us to move on.

Instead of the freedom, love, and safety I once felt at this church, a dense dark cloud of oppression moves in. I can feel it every time we walk in. We want church to be an experience with God, not full of hardships, doubts, gossip, and mistrust. Many of our friends and some leaders decide to leave as well. We are not alone in this feeling of displacement and loss. We set out to surround ourselves with a life-giving church family and live in a state of joy and trust.

Chapter 10

I decide that there is light at the end of every dark tunnel. I am not a hopeless case, or too crazy to figure things out. God sees me. He reaches down and lifts me up to a place of joy. He motivates me to continue working on myself and to connect with others. He shows me the truth about His love, and He does not walk away from me. I want to share this same joy with others.

"Cliff! Guess what just happened?" I say excitedly.

"What happened?" Cliff asks with a smile on his face.

"Okay, so I received a phone call from a woman in Maine. Apparently, she reads my blog and wants to know if I can go to Maine to speak at an event they are organizing for survivors of abuse!" I pause and take a breath then continue telling Cliff the thrilling news. "She says it doesn't have to be anything extensive. She also says that she feels God prompted her to reach out to me."

Cliff walks over to hug me and says, "Wow! That's incredible! It sounds very exciting."

"I know," I smile as I process all that God is doing. "It is more confirmation of God's promises in my life."

"When's the event?" he asks as he pours a soda into his mug.

"In one month. She says there is a dress code. I will need a black suit with a white blouse. I don't own anything like that, but I think I'll ask Ellie if she has something I can borrow," I tell him.

I ramble on about clothes, the plane trip, how much money they agreed to pay, and how it feels like confirmation from God working in my life and bring all things together in a fruitful way.

Cliff sips his soda as a slow smile spread across his face, "You are going to be great."

It feels exciting. When the woman calls and tells me she likes my blog and wants me to speak at her event, I can't believe it. After all the drama and loss, upon leaving the church, this feels like God is holding my hand and leading me to what I believe is my calling.

I begin to contemplate my upcoming talk. I want it to be interesting and, of course, I hope for others to be encouraged and feel loved. I swirl around several ideas and pray for God to guide me. He does just that! I come to a place of peace as I know without a doubt that Holy Spirit will provide the words for me at the right time. I don't have to stress about it.

A month later, I am on a plane heading to Maine for the event. The flight is long, and by the time I arrive, I am dead on my feet. "Hello, it's nice to meet you," Wanda holds out her hand and gives a friendly smile. "Dinner is waiting on the stove at home and a comfy bed."

I am grateful. "Hi! Thanks for coming to pick me up. I'm looking forward to this event, food, and a comfy bed." I tell her with a relaxed smile.

We leave the airport and drive to Wanda's house. It is late and dark, so I do not have a good look at the beautiful Maine landscape.

Wanda lives with her husband in a cute craftsman home located on five acres of land. We walk in the house and the smell of lentil soup with sour dough bread gives me a growly stomach. "It smells delicious." I comment.

She shows me to a sweet room with a double bed and cozy linens. The décor is in yellow and blue, with a warm hardwood floor and a braided rug. It is comfortable and welcoming.

"Make yourself at home; I'll go set the table and meet you out there." She turns to leave, and I unpack my bag. Then, without delay I meet her at the table and enjoy a warm delicious dinner. Feeling content ,I go back to the bedroom and collapse on the bed from jetlag and exhaustion.

The next day, Wanda and I meet up over a light breakfast. We get to know each other a bit and then head over to her workplace to meet the people in their group.

"I'll introduce you to some of the people, and then, if you don't mind too much, will you talk to the ladies in our groups? Most of them suffer from addictions or are victims of sexual abuse," Wanda says as we walk around the place.

"I would love to visit with them," I tell her.

After I talk to a few people, and meet ladies of the groups, I meet Wanda's boss. They arrange for us to have lunch together, so the day is spent reviewing the event, how they help the women, and what their organization is all about.

The next day is the event; I get some rest and prepare for the speech. As I get ready in the outfit I borrowed from Ellie,

I look at my reflection in the mirror and pray.

Whatever you want me to do and say, I am willing. I am also nervous. Be my words this evening and use me to speak to the hearts of others. Show yourself through the story I share. Just as he promised me earlier, I feel inspired and clear on everything I need to say.

The event is small and intimate, with about two hundred attendees. I am the keynote speaker, I feel honored. I'm excited to share with this group the power of God.

As the time approaches for me to go to the front, I feel the peace of God blanket me. Wanda introduces me, and I know deep within my heart that this moment in my life will be a time that marks a new spiritual beginning for me.

"Thank you for having me here this evening. I'm excited to share with you the path God has taken me on to find a place of healing," I say, and the audience smiles while some simply nod their heads in agreement.

"I'd like to share with you some of my life experiences. I'd like to begin with God has been asking me to speak for several years now. I am not a trained speaker; I don't always have a lot to say, which confirms to me even more that it is

God pulling me in this direction. So, I pray many times that God will speak through me and use me to shine in some way for Him," I can see many nods in agreement, and some with smiles on their faces.

I follow Holy Spirit's lead, starting with personal stories – stories of how I know deep within my heart that God speaks to me, how I have a deep desire to be in a committed relationship with Him and obey Him. Through all my struggles and trials, I can see that God is with me. I share stories of being a mother and the complete joy my children bring to my life and the loving way God gave me a man to marry that cherishes me and loves me unconditionally. I touch on how I struggled for many years to understand reality and truth from lies, and God now daily reveals to me that he is my reality.

At the end, my legs are like Jell-O. I feel emotionally spent, but happy at the same time. Women and some men talk to me after my speech. They tell me about their lives and struggles. Listening to them and helping is very satisfying.

"It went really well," I tell Cliff later that night as we talk about the event, and I give a run-by-run of my evening.

"I think the people connect with me on different levels. I think they left feeling like there is hope in God. I can't wait to get home, though. I've missed you!"

"I was confident it would go well! I think this is just another way of God telling you that He wants you to speak, and He will work it all out," Cliff responds.

As always, he has a lot of faith in me and my calling. He has no idea how much I appreciate his conviction that God uses me to encourage others.

***

After the success of my speech in Maine and my blog, I decide to start my own ministry. It is scary at first, but my friends and Cliff are there to bring support, and together we move forward.

Both Maddy and I start recovery groups for women who are suffering or have suffered in their life as I did. Maddy and I have grown a friendship on prayer and mutual respect, and love. We feel safe with each other. She did not waver in her support during the church trauma, and she is excited about being a part of our ministry and facilitating recovery groups with me.

Maddy is a huge help in the first women's retreat we plan where Hazel and I speak together, and I believe she will be there for many more events in the future.

A new chapter is beginning, one where we plan lots of events and connect with women. We build a team of like-minded women to help, and together we grow spiritually and emotionally. Clearly, God is leading me in this direction so I can continue to grow in who I am and who He is. The value of identity is a large focus for me and the ministry. I base my own identity on REAL. God wants me to be Rooted in him. He will Empower me as I lean more into faith. He will give me an Authentic life where I will Love and be Loved.

I put fear behind me and try new things. I focus on what God wants for me rather than what the people around me want me to do. Some things are more successful than others, but the main thing is God knows how to touch lives and my heart in all situations. To Him, this is success. I sometimes think about the time Hazel had predicted that I would not be fruitful in my endeavors, but I see that God turns life around, and not only does he give me a satisfying inner life, but He uses me in the lives of others to bring change. Even my friendship with Hazel proves to be a turning point for our journey. Our friendship tells the story of reconciliation and proves it is a work-in-progress, the effort is what counts.

With each day, I God is using my past to help others. The lies that once plagued my mind are turned into lessons of freedom. I am encouraged by the strength he has produces in me through trials. As I surrender all my thoughts to God, he changes my beliefs, perceptions, and I grow. I feel peace and gratefulness over the grace He gives me and the opportunities to speak into others' lives.

All of this gives me the ability and courage to acknowledge the impact of my past. If I dwell on dark thoughts, I become vulnerable and feel powerless. But when I see that through the power of God, I am strong and victorious. Without Him, I am weak. I admit that God shows me my value and weaves truth in my heart as I lean on him. I sense there are areas of unforgiveness in my heart, but I believe God will lead me to find relief as I progress.

I am grateful and encouraged for the friends God places in my life, and even though I am cautious and not readily open about my history, I believe He brings deep connections to me at the times I need them most. I am blessed with friendships that develop from the groups I taught at church, and friendships through my own ministry. Loyal friends like Kayla and Lani endure the test of time and trials. I am thankful to God for answering my prayer and bringing loyal, kind women into my life.

My relationship with Hazel and Maddy grows closer, and I am freer to share myself without fear of rejection. Women from the previous groups I did at church are in my life as friends now, and I am greatly enriched by them.

Similarly, Abigail and I meet regularly. We have a common bond of once being together in the same church community, then searching elsewhere. I feel fortunate to have so many friends and recognize that God answers my prayer for wise women daily. The reconciliation between Hazel and I strengthen my faith in God.

God has given me the strength to trust others again. Trust is not quick, and I find myself listening more than talking, but I begin to believe that these are the friends that will stay. Surrender to Him gives me the freedom I always had available but didn't know how to get. The feeling of living in a cage no longer haunts me, for I can see that the cage was the pain of my past and the lies of believing I was trapped. He leads me to the light, and I follow his lead, no matter where it takes me.

Chapter 11

The passing of time brings joys and challenges, all leading to stronger bonds with each other and a deep gratefulness for the gift of life, family, and friends. Through the years, I go through phases and times. Usually, I live in a state of unbridled hope, grasping the power of surrender and peace. Sometimes, I am challenged with self-doubt, questions without answers, and flickers of depression.

With each difficulty, I take it to God and express every thought and feeling. I trust that there is nothing I can say that will cause God to leave me. He comforts me with strength and compassion to traverse every situation. Cliff and I go through some tough times that give us the opportunity to lean heavily into the truth of Jesus and His people. It starts with a few health problems.

Cliff suffers from pain in his hip that is so intense he can barely walk. I begin to get abdominal pain that is also high in intensity and leaves me doubled over. We pray to God and push through the pain and wait for a breakthrough. Both of us seek medical attention and answers.

"How did it go at the doctor's office today?" I ask Cliff as he hobbles into the kitchen with his bad hip.

"They took an X-ray and examined my hip. He says it is arthritis. Eventually, I may need a hip replacement. "He tells me.

"But what about now? You're in so much pain!" I express my concern.

"I don't know. I'm going to keep praying about it," he says.

As weeks go by, we both focus on prayer for Cliff's hip and his pain.

"I believe God is telling me to stop drinking soda," Cliff announces one day.

"Really? No more Mountain Dew? You love it.! That is an interesting request, don't you think? What does soda have to do with anything?" I reply with a small smile.

"I'm going to take a break and see if there's anything to it," he proclaims. Cliff stays true to his word and makes considerable changes to his diet, including the soda boycott.

And much to my surprise and relief, the pain dissipates. We are both in awe that God spoke such a simple solution. Upon research we discover that sugary soda increases inflammation, which causes pain!

"My hip doesn't hurt anymore! God actually brought the thought to stop soda to my mind so I would feel better!" he exclaims in happiness.

"It is incredible, really," I say as I hug him. I tuck the incident away in my mind, believing it was a miracle. I remind myself that there will be future events that will require me to look back on all that God has done and remember his goodness. I wonder what else God will bless us with…

God is a living presence in our lives. And with each day, both Cliff and I surrender ourselves to Him and enjoy who He is. His constant support and love leave me humbled and brings me to my knees. I understand that the trials of life made us stronger. And because of the pain, questions, and despair that I so often felt, I now support others and give them hope.

The flashes and visions of my past are a distant memory,

and I feel at peace. I am grounded, in the place that God has brought me to. I enjoy the ministry, my friends, reconciling and rebuilding my bond with Hazel, as well as my family. The three older boys are grown up with families of their own by now, and it brings me joy and pride to watch them. I praise God daily for raising them to be such strong and loving men.

Cliff, as always, is my rock through all these years. He has a strong faith and relies on God to see him through his own struggles. The miracle of his hip relief brings him to a new level of faith and reliance on God. Our relationship remains steadfast. He stays by my side in the difficult times, and the joyful times. And now, we are stronger together.

The abdominal pain is now unbearable, and I'm doubled over and clutching my stomach as tears stream down my face. "I'm in so much pain! I feel like I'm in labor all the time." I am seeing a doctor, but he does not know what the issue is. Both Cliff and I pray for relief. "God, what is going on?! Please, help me!" I cry out to Him.

The doctor, Justin, finally suggests exploratory surgery, and I agree without hesitation. I check in to the hospital early one morning on the day my surgery is scheduled.

"Bethany, it looks like the veins in your stomach are twisted around your uterus and one ovary, consequently causing you tremendous pain. The solution here is to have another surgery and remove the uterus and the ovary that is being squeezed." Doctor Justin explains to me. "We will need to submit the paperwork to your insurance, and as soon as they approve, we can schedule the surgery."

"How long will that take?" I inquire.

"A week at most," is the response.

A week goes by in a blur after that diagnosis, and I have yet to receive any news or call from the doctor regarding my pending surgery. I will wait a couple more days before contacting them myself.

"Your insurance will not approve the surgery," the assistant says over the phone.

"What? Why? What's the next step?" I feel anger inside me.

"We have to resubmit the application and Doctor Justin will appeal," the kind assistant tries to ease my tension.

"And how long will that take?" I ask.

"Could be a couple of months," she answers.

I have questions. So many of them. How am I going to get through this physical pain and continue with life? Will God heal this too? Our medical bills pile up. Our business is losing clients, and we don't see a lot of profit. Our finances are drained. I am exhausted as I consider what the next few months might entail.

I open my journal. *"God, you bring me through so much. I choose to believe you will give me the strength to walk through this as well. The pain, at times, makes it very difficult for me to function. I can't do this day in and day out and be there for my family. Please help me! I give my body to you."*

Eight months later, the surgery is approved by our insurance. I finally go to the hospital for my surgery, which is going to be a big one.

"Can you come and pray with me before I go into the operating room?" I ask Doctor Justin.

"Absolutely, I'd be happy to," he smiles at me reassuringly.

The surgery is a success, and I wake up feeling an

immediate difference. However, my recovery proves to be difficult. The day I come home from the hospital; Hazel comes to visit us. She brings us dinner, and I am grateful for the help. But then, as the evening progresses, I feel worse, and I cannot breathe without intense pain. With each breath, there is a croaking noise, as if there is a frog in my chest.

"I need to lie down. I can't breathe, and it hurts," I gasp.

Cliff and Hazel help me to the bedroom.

"I think we need to call the doctor," Hazel looks worriedly at Cliff.

He dials the number on his phone hurriedly. The doctor that is available on call asks me a few questions. Then he tells me to get to the emergency room right away.

"It might be a blood clot." He warns me.

As Cliff and I rush to the hospital, Hazel tells us she will stay behind with our son and daughter.

"My wife is here for some pain in her chest. The doctor advised us to come in." Cliff explains to the receptionist.

"Yes, your doctor called ahead. We are ready for you," she says quickly.

They rush me to a room and help me on the examination table. The room is instantly filled with doctors and nurses who all work quickly to prep medical equipment.

"What's your pain level?" the nurse asks.

"I'm at an eight or a nine," I whisper, unable to speak due to the pain.

"We will give you something for the pain and relax you," she explains to me.

Immediately, I can feel the drugs take effect.

"It takes the edge off," I tell the nurse as she gently touches my hand.

"It doesn't appear to be a blood clot so, that's good news," the emergency room doctor says. "But it does look like you were not given proper treatment after the surgery, and there is a lot of gas left in your abdomen. This is extremely painful. We are going to give you some pain meds via IV. We'll keep you here for a couple of days for observation as well."

I feel relief oozing through my veins, as I drift off to sleep. In the next couple of days, I am plagued with nightmares and yelling voices in the distance. I cannot wake up. Finally, I pull myself into a conscious state. Cliff holds my hand, Abigail and Don gaze at me from the foot of the bed, and my daughter-in-law, Pearl, looks on nervously from a nearby chair.

"What happened?" I ask

"The nurse gave you too much pain medication, and it knocked you out for two days straight. The doctor tried several things to wake you up, including banging on your chest with his fists. You have some bruises from that. We are so relieved to see you awake!" Cliff gently kisses my forehead.

I drift in and out of sleep. Friends and family check on me, but most of the time I am unaware of their presence. I finally get to go home. I am grateful for life. The episode is so bizarre to me. I feel angry at the incompetence of the nurse that overdosed me. Still, I remember God's power and believe that He was there with me the entire time. I come to Him with questions, hoping that my trust in Him will only grow by asking them.

"Can I question God and still trust Him?" I ask Cliff. "Because I do it all the time." I feel a little sheepish.

"I think questioning Him is a sure sign of trust," he says.

Health issues and physical pain continue to plague me. I go through months of surgeries and physical therapy for frozen shoulders, bone spurs, tendonitis, etc. I continue to have faith and trust in God, for I know that he does not fail me. His promises for love, peace, and hope keep me.

The recession brings dire financial complications, and we are forced to sell our home and other investments we have built up. Cliff and I cling to each other desperately during these times, knowing that we only have each other and God. Our business, which we put our heart and soul into, keeps decreasing, it is our main source of income, and has been for years. We are near the brink of loss and bankruptcy but still cling to each other and to God.

We desperately look for ways to thank God, even though we see it all wither away financially. We are grateful for the home provided to us and consider it to be a retreat away from the noise of the city. No matter how serious and life-threatening, our faith in God remains steady through all our hardships and struggles in life. And our faith does not disappoint. Time and time again, we witness and observe as God saves us and protects us through every crisis and struggle. He rescues us and keeps us safe.

Friends leave money on our doorstep or bring us food when we cannot purchase groceries. God continues to use our family and friends to bring love and support to us. We turn to God in prayer and gratefulness for all that He provides, even when it feels like we are losing and going backward.

Many small businesses around us begin to fail, but just when we think we cannot make it another day, God brings us a new client or a check in the mail. One morning, while praying, I hear the word "Prosper" in my mind. I complain to God that I do not feel we are at a place of prospering right now, but I will claim it as my word. A few days later, Cliff receives a call from a man named Prosper. He and his company give us enough business to get us through the next year! Again, I am in awe at the way God works in our lives. I am grateful that our children can witness His power and see the ways He provides for us. We are never without food on the table or a bed to sleep in, and a roof over our heads.

Through all the tough times, God keeps us going. On paper it looks impossible, but with God it works out. He promises to take care of the ones that love him. It gives us renewed hope, love, faith, courage, and peace. We continue to live well, thanks to His grace and miracles.

Chapter 12

P
eace can be surprising. We spend all our lives trying everything we can to achieve it. And then, without realizing it, peace parks itself inside our hearts as if it always lived there. Peace comes quietly, gently, like a soft blanket on a cold winter day.

When we nurture a relationship with Jesus, peace is stitched into all aspects of life. It's warm and inviting, and it gives a heart of gratitude. Perspective changes. Much of my life is one of pain, sadness, shame, guilt, fear, and even anger. However, when I surrender the pain, sadness, shame, guilt, fear, and anger to God, I find the truth of peace. Years of misery and struggles led me to peace. For me, peace came with the acceptance of who God is, who he says I am, forgiving others and myself, and focused on God as my reality.

God is faithful to me. The moment I begin to root myself into the character and love of Jesus, life changes. It changes because he empowers me to change. The deeper I dig into his presence, the more empowered I become. When I dig, I become authentic. I worked hard for a long time to keep my secrets. I didn't want my friends to know about Frank or my childhood. I told myself that I needed to protect my children from knowing as well. But living in secret creates a wall and it is difficult to be authentic. With my story, I am free to be authentic. With these factors I believe that I can love others and be loved. Love is blind to a multitude of sins; it covers us and heals us. Love is God and there is power in the acceptance of love. Love also knows boundaries, and when we love ourselves, we know when to say goodbye to toxic relationships.

The path is long and difficult. Truth always prevails when we choose to take its path. When I choose to tell my story, I walk in truth, I am choosing to rise above the pain and hardships and be a witness of God's healing power. This, in turn, creates a strong bond with faithful friends and loving family. It gives me so much more to be grateful for.

A meaningful relationship in my life is my friendship with Hazel. Our friendship has its ups and downs. We started on a rocky stage but gradually, with the help of God, got closer. We spend more time with each other, God guiding me to remain close to her.

I believe God put Hazel and me in each other's lives for a reason. I enjoyed her company for a season, and for that I am grateful. I still marvel at the God who stitched us together in a deep spirited friendship. I learned a lot from Hazel. She taught me many things without realizing it. I learned how to be, as well as how *not* to be. The practice of friendship with Hazel blessed me immensely.

When I decide to pen down my experiences and write a book based on my life story, I approach her. I ask Hazel if she wants to participate and give her input on the book. Since she is such a big part of my life, including her seems essential. But my desire to write about my life events and express how the wounds of God's people can greatly impact us for good and evil, are not shared by Hazel.

It sets off a chain of events and Hazel starts to withdraw from me. The time that we do spend together has gaps of silence and unsaid expectations. Our friendship suffers, with an underlying anger and bitter regret, and we grow distant. Soon enough, the trust and faith in our friendship erodes, and we lose the closeness we had spent so long to build. She believes that if I write a book, it will hurt her and so she asks me to write about something else.

Initially, I am deeply saddened by Hazel's response. I consider keeping everything a secret. I grieve over the choice I feel I must make. Cliff and I talk about it extensively, and he encourages me to write what I can and reminds me that it is a book about my life, not Hazel's.

When I turn to God, I seek answers to my troubles. I ask Him what to do about the situation and how to speak the truth in a way that shows his grace but doesn't reflect anything vicious towards another. I ask Him to guide me.

He leads me to realize that this book is about my experience. It is about my life and the experiences that I gain, whether good or bad. These experiences make me who I am today, and I cannot shy away from them. I also cannot refuse to acknowledge them when it comes to a book about my own life.

I choose not to let anyone tell me or emotionally coerce me into living a life far from the truth. No matter how horrible and painful, these life experiences allow me to find safety and refuge in Jesus.

I once struggled to find my identity. To understand who I am and what I am. My journey brings me to understand that

God has forgiven me, therefore I will forgive others. I am reconciled with Christ. I am known by him, and he sees me for who I really am. I believe He wants me to speak of my experiences and walk forward in faith.

He chooses me and justifies my existence. Because of him, I am alive, saved, accepted, and free. Even though my experiences helped me reach this point in life, they do not define me. I am not the pain that I suffered or the abuse I encountered.

God is my identity, not the pain of my past. Thanks to him, I have security, love, and peace. He loves me and makes me a new being – a new person. I belong to Him, born by Him, and adopted by Him. I am a child of promise and friend of Jesus Christ. My true home is not in the house I live in on earth; it is heaven. I am a daughter of the King. I am sealed in Him and loved by Him.

That is my identity, the one that Christ gives me. And that is what I want to portray in my book—the beauty of all that I have learned and walk through in my relationship with God. I want to people understand and see the reality of their identity, the identity that Christ has given them.

As you know, I enjoy writing. I have years of journals as my witness. It is one of the ways I communicate with God. It also is a tool I can use to minister to other people. Writing has given me a voice and enables others to see God through my words. It helps them learn about themselves, which is precisely what I hope to achieve through this book.

Writing in my blog, has allows me to be a beacon of hope not just to others but also to myself. With the help of writing, I make sense of what is going on inside my head. I can untangle my thoughts and emotions by writing them down one by one. It is my method of prayer, and an instrument of hope.

With this book, I pray that I can share with others the same hope, peace, awareness, knowledge, and understanding that I have received from God's words.

My life is not without pain, the difference now is I have God to pave a way. Recently I was diagnosed with cancer. Stage three. At times it was a very long road to recovery, but the one thing consistent during that time is the faithfulness of God. I decided in the beginning to never claim cancer as part of my identity. Cancer does not have the power to say who I am. Not only has God assured me that I will have a long life, but he told numerous others to share that promise with me. I am happy to say that I am now cancer free. I did have chemo and radiation, yet still, I credit God for his healing power in my life. He is Rapha, he heals. I am a walking miracle in more ways than one. We all are in one way or another.

When the Church Thinks You're Crazy

You now hold the keys to peace, health, joy, and identity. By sharing your honest opinion of this book on Amazon, you can help others find the same freedom and understanding you've gained.

Your review could be the light another reader—one who may be struggling with abuse or trapped in a toxic relationship—needs to find hope and healing. Each word you share can guide someone toward the support they're searching for, helping to keep the healing alive and growing.

Thank you for being part of this journey and for helping me continue this work. Together, we're lighting the path for others.

Leave Review

https://bethanyelle.com/amazonlaunch

Epilogue

As a trauma coach, ministry leader, speaker, and author, I have the platform to share my story and hear the beautiful stories of others.

I get to meet and be inspired by women who have survived abuse by those in power, many of them have the heartache of betrayal by a church body or have faced the devastating loss of friendship. We stand together and are not alone!

I have made friends with many of these women. And for this book, friends have lent me their voices and stories. They agree to share their thoughts and feelings in their own words so I can include them in this book. I support them with all my heart, and hopefully, their stories will help you find peace and inspiration as well.

Charlotte's Story

When we take on Jesus' name, we are called to live in deep agape love and integrity. One of the greatest lessons I have learned from my friend, Bethany, is the weightiness of words. The responsibility of speaking thoughtlessly, the importance of backing up our promises with our actions. Like the ripple effect from a stone tossed into a pool of water, when we fail to act in love, church hurts can impact bystanders in ways we may never realize.

I was a bystander, never directly injured by a church, but affected by the hurt received by another. When I signed up for a workshop that was being held at a church, my childhood faith was in a dormant state. Over those twelve weeks, I saw joy in the eyes of Bethany, the co-facilitator, which intrigued and drew me. She gently challenged my unwillingness to commit to Jesus fully. When I puzzled over what God might want me to do in any given situation, she would always ask, "Did you ask Him?"

After our class ended, she offered to meet me for a coffee every week. I loved our meetings; my brain came away feeling stretched with new possibilities. But early on, as I decided to start attending church every week, she told me she might be leaving soon. I never knew the extent of what she was facing. She was too cautious about venting. I was too self-absorbed to ask many questions.

I wanted to join a small group but felt hesitant to walk into a houseful of strangers. So, she invited me to join the group she and her husband hosted. Around their long table, in a room full of food and laughter and later Bible study, I found a loving family in my small group.

I tagged along as Bethany delivered meals and empathetic hugs to a woman recovering from painful surgery. And because I lived quite a distance away, she invited me to stay with her family on Saturday nights. So, I got to see her at home, always with the same consistency, integrity and deeply lived faith as in public.

I came to a new believer's joy, a commitment to Christ, regular attendance at a church, and baptism. Because of the faithful example of Bethany pointing to Jesus, when she no longer felt welcome there, I chose to leave too.

She assured me that I did not need to make that choice out of loyalty to her. But I did feel both loyalty to my friend, and wariness toward a Body that was rejecting her instead of embracing her gifts. It was disillusioning.

Did that church Body lose because one bystander walked away? I think so. Even if it is the smallest tithe or a smile at the weary stranger in the next chair, I think we all have something to contribute. I trust none of it has been in vain. My closest friends have all suffered church hurts and grown stronger in their faith, despite it. Christ never intended us to wound our fellow believers.

Even when Bethany was not welcome, or was in the midst of deep pain, she came to this particular body if it meant showing them the love of Jesus. Isn't that what we should all do to love like Jesus?

Drew's Story

We were the family that had it all. Larry was a successful businessman, community leader, and an elder of a mega Christian church. I was dedicated to supporting Larry's success, raising our four children, running our ample home, while entertaining church, community, and friends. The children were busy doing all the expected activities that thriving, well-rounded children need to grow into proper adults.

I should have recognized the signs much earlier in our marriage. Larry was an accomplished chameleon, and I had remained as naive as I was the day we met. Larry became increasingly angry and withdrawn. He lost control of his business, selling it for a fraction of its previous worth. He accepted a temporary job as an administrator of our church. He was becoming moodier and more unpredictable.

The church position ended, and Larry fell into a deep depression. For four months, he left the bedroom only to gulp down a glass of milk and hand me lists of medications he required from the drugstore.

I found telltale signs of porn, sexual perversion, and adultery. He started hallucinating, seeing, and hearing people who weren't there. I was confused and afraid. I talked with the church leaders who he had worked with for years. They all told me that they sensed something was "off" with his behavior but wouldn't elaborate. Not comforting. Even less helpful, I was told to "stand by my man."

Frightened, I focused on protecting myself and my children while the leadership tried, unsuccessfully, to do interventions. I wasn't getting anywhere with the church leaders, and Larry was slipping from bad to worse. The children were afraid to be alone in the house with him. After about nine months of bizarre behavior, Larry decided to leave our home. I was numb.

I cried...literally...to our homegroup. Each week in the confidence of our fellowship, I shared my heartbreaking discoveries. They held me and tried to help me make sense of what was happening.

Larry said he wanted a divorce. He was cussing more heavily, and I feared for our children. Our oldest daughter had become suicidal, and the other three were acting out in their own ways. Larry didn't seem surprised when I said I wanted sole custody.

One day, two friends from my home group asked me out to lunch. I had just returned from visiting my suicidal daughter in the hospital. She had shared some of her experiences with her dad. Thankful for the chance to temporarily escape my nightmare, I met them at my favorite restaurant.

We had scarcely ordered when the real reason for their invitation became apparent. They began to present Larry's case, stating what a good father Larry was and why we should have joint custody. I felt ambushed. Never had I suspected such a motive or tactic from my home group friends.

I left the restaurant, my meal untouched. A few weeks later, while helping a homegroup member move, the group laughed together as they recounted how much fun they had at a family outing with Larry and his girlfriend. Girlfriend? We weren't even divorced yet!

My stomach ached, and my head reeled. How could they betray me like this? They had seen my anguish. They had watched my world collapse. With all the strength I could muster, I excused myself from the homegroup forever.

I left the megachurch to attend a small church led by our former community pastor. So did the members of my old home group. In this small congregation, I was faced with my former friends and confidants every Sunday. It was a painful reminder of betrayal on many levels. But my children had found the love and support they needed in the church's youth group. I felt trapped.

My weekly prayer time with Bethany and our faithful friendship to each other kept me going day to day. Through the toughest of times, we walked with each other and found solace in each other's loyal companionship.

As months went by, God started to work the thought of forgiveness into the thick, protective armor that encased my heart. I wanted nothing to do with it. It was all too terribly painful.

God is patient. He waited seven long years as He healed me and strengthened my faith. Then, He presented me with the ultimate forgiveness sermon. By the end of the message, I knew that I had completely forgiven my friends and that I must now tell them and ask their forgiveness. I made my way over to them and explained how hurt I had been.

As we hugged, my friend explained that she hadn't wanted to hurt me, but Larry had needed them more. I knew it was true. I was glad they were there for him.

I feel no more anger or pain in our friendship. The Body of Christ is once again a place of peace and joyful worship. I have friends who love and support me. I love and support them too. God's love has reconciled us to Him and each other.

In my years of hearing story after story, I relate to each one on some level, I have seen that we all walk through difficult times. We are all searching for the depth of who God created us to be. We all want to be seen, heard, and loved.

When we believe that our experience grows us, but does not define us, we let go of the shame and grasp the truth of who God proclaims us to be.

I'm excited and nervous about sharing my story with you. I thank my friends for being bold enough to share theirs. Most of all, I hope there is something you can grab ahold of in the words I have shared with you that give you hope and maybe even direction.

So, as I come to the end of the pages of my book, a book that gives you a glimpse into a portion of my life, I want to leave you with a prayer and ask for your positive review. Please go to Amazon and share your thoughts on this journey.

God, Jesus, and Holy Spirit

I humbly come before you and praise you for every detail of life. In times of stress and pain, I praise You because you lead us and teach us along the way. In the times of joy, I praise You because you show truth and bring us all to places of reality in you. I know you are good because of Your immense love for us and for all your people. Thank you for courage. Thank you for life. Thank you for forgiveness and for being the way to eternal life. I give myself to you in complete surrender, and I believe that you have created me to be a world-changer.

The End

www.ingramcontent.com/pod-product-compliance
Lightning Source LLC
Chambersburg PA
CBHW071159130626
46553CB00004B/1713